Praise for
Subscription Marketing

"Keeping an existing customer is much more profitable than selling a new one, especially in a subscription business. Today's real-time communications environment makes a subscription model incredibly lucrative for those who know how to navigate the new rules—just ask the likes of Google, Netflix, and Amazon.com. Anne Janzer shows you how to implement value nurturing of existing and potential clients that will drive your success in this new world."

David Meerman Scott
Best-selling author of *The New Rules of Marketing and PR*, now in 25 languages from Arabic to Vietnamese

"Anne's terrific new book is an excellent primer to help your business take advantage of the subscription economy, while navigating around potential potholes. And as a bonus: It's clear, straightforward, and refreshingly jargon-free!"

Ann Handley
Chief Content Officer, MarketingProfs, and author of the WSJ best seller, *Everybody Writes*

"The Subscription Economy is changing the nature of the customer–vendor relationship, and that has major implications for marketing organizations. *Subscription Marketing* offers creative and practical strategies to keep the subscriber front and center in your marketing efforts."

Brian Bell
Chief Marketing Officer, Zuora

"Although there is no 'holy grail' measurement for content marketing, there is one that sits atop the rest—the subscriber. As more organizations move from paid to owned media, acquiring and keeping subscribers to our information is more important than ever. This is critical to your business. Read Anne's book and you'll have everything you need to create and execute a subscription strategy that works."

Joe Pulizzi
Founder, Content Marketing Institute, and
author, *Epic Content Marketing*

"In today's marketing organizations customer success and customer engagement have never been more important. Creating compelling marketing programs for the new subscription economy is an exciting opportunity for teams willing to learn and take on the challenge."

John Robb
Entrepreneur, former VMware General Manager

"It's one thing to bring new customers in the front door, but if you're losing too many out the back door, your growth could be severely hampered, could stall, or worse. The best subscription companies work diligently to ensure their subscribers continually realize value so they stay customers for a long time, increase spending over time, and bring in other customers along the way. Anne's book will help you do that, too."

Lincoln Murphy
Customer Success Evangelist at Gainsight and
founder of Sixteen Ventures

"The subscription economy calls for a new type of marketer—one who focuses on nurturing customers, making them successful, and creating ongoing value. This book illustrates the impact marketing can have in engaging users and driving customer success. It's a good read for marketers who want to step up to a broader role in the modern enterprise."

Kaiser Mulla-Feroze
Chief Marketing Officer, Totango

"Over the past five years, every marketing organization has been turned on its head. The rise of subscription business models combined with new customer engagement channels are forcing marketing professionals into uncharted territory. Author Anne Janzer does an outstanding job of detailing the new realities of value-based marketing in a subscription-dominated world. A must-read for every marketing organization, *Subscription Marketing* reveals the secrets and strategies for engaging and keeping customers for life."

Randy Brasche
Senior Director of Corporate Marketing at
ServiceSource

"The role of marketing comes down to three words: Make sales easier. If it doesn't initiate the sales cycle, shorten it, or make repeat sales easier, don't do it. Janzer's excellent book focuses on the third—and most overlooked—component of this equation. It's required reading for anyone trying to maximize their marketing budget—which is everyone."

Tom Hogan
Founder and Principal, Crowded Ocean

"The subscription economy runs not just on value creation; it runs on value nurturing. As Anne Janzer's book *Subscription Marketing* deftly outlines, successful subscription management leads to increased lifetime values *only if* customers realize promised value from your offerings. Filled with great examples across industries, this book is a well-written and easy 'must-read' on why and how to add value for both subscriptions and non-subscription-based services alike."

Kathy Klotz-Guest
Marketing storyteller, improviser, and
founder, Keeping it Human, Inc.

"Marketing is about making people care about your product or service enough to want to talk it up to others and become brand advocates. Anne's book reminds us that many marketers forget about the customer once the sale is made and the real value in any customer is in continuing to nurture them through value marketing. *Subscription Marketing* outlines fantastic examples of how marketers can learn value nurturing and apply it to their existing marketing tactics to increase business value. No matter where you are in your marketing career, you'll definitely get a few nuggets out of this book."

Tracy Sestili
CEO Social Strand Media, and author of
Taking Your Brand from the Bench to the Playing Field

"Marketing for subscription customers is about long-term relationships and experience, not short-term wins. You can't afford to take your eyes off the customer experience, even long after the sale. In *Subscription Marketing*, Anne points out that subscription marketers need to continually nurture customer value. The strategies in this book can help you build marketing practices that engage your customers while minimizing churn for better business results."

Lisa Abbott
Product Marketing Director, Genesys

STRATEGIES FOR NURTURING
CUSTOMERS IN A WORLD OF CHURN

SUBSCRIPTION
MARKETING

Anne H. Janzer

Contents

Introduction

Welcome to the Subscription Economy

Over the course of a typical week, my life is fairly simple. With breakfast, I read the *New York Times* online and do the crossword puzzle. In my home office, I check email, then fire up Microsoft Word and start working. I work out at the local YMCA. I might go to Costco to pick up a few things. Evenings often feature a television show recorded on TiVo or a movie streamed from Netflix or Amazon Prime. I'll read a book on my Kindle before going to sleep.

As simple as they sound, these activities are made possible by multiple subscription relationships that I, as a consumer, maintain with various businesses:

- *New York Times* subscription
- Broadband data subscription
- Google Apps subscription (for my email)
- Office 365 for Word
- YMCA annual membership
- Costco annual membership
- TiVo and Netflix subscriptions
- Amazon prime membership

These are just a few of the many ongoing subscriptions in my life. You likely have dozens of subscriptions, perhaps more than you realize.

The number of subscription relationships we manage is constantly growing. New technologies enable subscription services for products as constant as socks and underwear. Beyond consumer goods and services, the subscription model is reshaping how businesses purchase everything from software for running operations to chemicals used in manufacturing.

As businesses adopt subscription models for selling their goods and services, marketing organizations need to adapt. The strategies that marketers have used for years to make one-time sales fall short when the customer relationship continues over time. The subscription economy will change the practice of marketing.

We're All Participants in the Subscription Economy

This book uses the term *subscription* to refer to any type of recurring revenue model in which the customer chooses regularly and repeatedly to remain a customer. In this sense, a subscription may refer to:

- Services to which customers actively subscribe
- Pay-as-you-go pricing for cloud-based software
- Managed services in the industrial context
- Membership fees for communities or purchasing programs
- Regularly scheduled purchases of physical or digital goods

Nearly every industry now participates in the emerging subscription economy. Even if your own business doesn't have a subscription component, your competitors probably do.

Although the business model is old, recent years have seen subscription-based offerings invade new markets. New technologies are driving much of this change. Appropriately, the technology industry is among the first to be significantly disrupted by subscriptions (in the form of cloud computing).

Working with high tech companies as a marketing consultant, I've had the opportunity to watch firsthand the impact of subscriptions on the software industry. Business models have evolved, but marketing practices haven't changed much. Even as revenue streams shift to recurring revenues from existing customers, many marketing organizations focus primarily on generating leads and closing initial sales.

In traditional business models, marketing and sales organizations worry about losing *new* sales to competitors. In a subscription economy, all your current customers are fair game for competitors. Because customers pay as they go, they constantly make the decision to remain a customer (renew) or leave for a competitor (churn). With no up-front, capital investment in your business, they may be easily tempted to switch.

> In the subscription economy, you're only doing half of your job as a marketer if you focus simply on making the sale and ignore the customer.

Marketing Practices Are Shifting

The growth of subscription models isn't happening in a vacuum. Marketers are dealing with seismic shifts as traditional marketing tactics based on interruption and information scarcity lose effectiveness.

The practice of marketing is changing. If you studied marketing in school, you learned the 4 P's of the marketing mix (product, place, price, promotion.) Then you enter a world of inbound marketing, SEO, social media strategy, mobile apps, gamification, content marketing, video marketing, and countless other trends. The real marketing mix is a swirling alphabet soup.

Interruption is less effective. People are losing patience with marketing techniques that interrupt them, such as pop-up ads, television ads, and phone calls. Faced with a flood of content, marketing organizations have to find new ways to get the attention of prospects.

The balance of power is shifting. Marketing and salespeople aren't the keepers of product or service truth and insight anymore. Customers can find detailed information, including recommendations and reviews, before they ever contact your business or visit your website.

Trust in business is eroding. According to the 2014 Edelman Trust Barometer, trust in corporate leadership is low worldwide.

> Only one in four General Public respondents trust business leaders to correct issues and even fewer— one in five—to tell the truth and make ethical and moral decisions.[1]

People are growing disillusioned with businesses that chase short-term profits at the expense of societal and environmental values. And as the customer-facing part of the business, marketing bears the brunt of that mistrust.

Marketing to Customers after the Sale

Traditional marketing strategies and techniques are crafted toward the initial sale, turning prospects into customers. In a subscription business, marketing organizations need to shift their focus from the point of sale to the long-term, ongoing customer relationship. The subscription customer must decide, repeatedly, to remain a customer or your business will not succeed. In effect, the customer remains a prospect, deserving ongoing engagement and nurturing.

This book suggests that marketers add a core objective to their practices: *value nurturing*. Value nurturing happens after the initial sale. Its objective is to help the customer achieve and realize value from the solution. In the subscription economy, value nurturing lasts much longer than lead generation and nurturing.

Value nurturing serves your long-term business interests. Customers who realize value are likely to renew their subscriptions; competitors must work much harder to lure them away. These customers may also purchase more from your business, whether by upgrading or buying other services. And the most loyal customers refer others to your business.

Ultimately, this shift in marketing practices works to everyone's advantage. Customers benefit when businesses take their long-term interests to heart and help them achieve sustained success. Effective value nurturing makes customers happier and more successful. And we are all somebody's customers.

How to Use This Book

This book is intended for anyone involved in a marketing role in a business that relies on a subscription model for some or all of its revenues.

The examples here span business-to-business (B2B) and business-to-consumer (B2C) companies in diverse industries. As the subscription business model expands, Fortune 100 corporations and scrappy start-ups may have more in common than they realize. Rather than looking at what your competitors are doing today, I want to help you cast a wider net in considering what will work for your business and customers.

Part One describes what's happening in the subscription shift across industries and how those changes affect marketing. It examines the challenges of managing multiple business models, as well as the limitations of practices based on a linear sales funnel. This section defines the marketing practice of *value nurturing*—helping your customers realize value from the subscription-based offering.

Part Two includes examples of value nurturing strategies. From B2B giants to consumer companies, the examples highlight a variety of ideas for all facets of value nurturing, including:

- Helping customers achieve success
- Demonstrating to your customers the value that they are achieving
- Adding value outside the solution through content, community, ecosystems, and other strategies
- Adding value to the customer relationship

- Helping customers express and realize their own values by defining, communicating, and sharing story and purpose

Part Three offers suggestions for putting the strategies in Part Two into practice. Topics include building the business case to get buy-in and integrating value nurturing with existing marketing tools and programs. Finally, I offer four guidelines as a value-based marketing manifesto:

1. Empathize with your customers
2. Show your personality
3. Handle your mistakes with grace
4. Don't be creepy

If you already understand the impact of the subscription business model on your business, spend time perusing the strategies in Part Two. If you want to convince others of the need for action, you'll find the ammunition you need in Part One and metrics for building a business case in Part Three.

No matter how your business participates in the subscription economy, the ideas in this book should inspire you to take your marketing to the next level, and have fun while doing it.

If you want to explore the topic beyond the book, visit the Resources page on the book website: www.SubscriptionMarketingBook.com/resources. Enter your email to join the subscription marketing group and download related resources.

Part One:
The Subscription Shift

Chapter 1:

The Growing Subscription Economy

Charles Dickens published his novels as serial installments in Victorian England. *The Pickwick Papers* installments were *The Sopranos* of the day. The subscription business model itself has been around at least as long as the first magazines or newspapers.

Technology makes new types of subscriptions possible and practical by simplifying access and distribution. I can subscribe to Google Shopping Express and have my groceries delivered. Instead of buying movies, I subscribe to Netflix and either stream videos or borrow DVDs, without leaving home. Other services can keep me supplied with razors, wine, pet food, and socks. Even Amazon Prime is a subscription.

In the business world, the subscription model is reshaping how businesses purchase everything from software to storage, telecommunications, printing, personnel services, supplies, chemicals, and more. The change is more pervasive than you may realize.

Early subscription models had a personal quality—you knew the person who delivered your paper or brought your order of milk. I spoke with someone recently who remembered milk being delivered by a horse-drawn cart. The horse knew which houses to stop at and walked ahead of the milkman making the deliveries. Now *that's* personalized service.

Businesses are taking advantage of web-based and mobile technologies to personalize subscriptions at scale. Subscription-based businesses are gradually transforming many industries. Industries from retail shopping to industrial supplies are up for grabs as part of the evolving subscription shift.

Finding Patterns in the Clouds

For an object lesson in how subscriptions transform and disrupt industries, look no further than software companies.

In the technology industry, software led the shift to subscriptions. Using Software as a Service (SaaS), you don't have to buy packaged software, nor do you need to own the hardware to run the software. Salesforce pioneered the business-oriented SaaS market, giving companies of all sizes access to advanced Customer Relationship Management (CRM) software that previously was expensive and complex to implement. Today Salesforce revenues exceed four billion dollars annually. The CRM market has been transformed.

Software as a Service is one part of the broader cloud computing market. The term *cloud computing* refers to using networked computing resources over the Internet rather than local computer resources to store or manage data and applications. Developers can use Platform as a Service (PaaS) to build apps. Infrastructure as a Service (IaaS) offers on-demand access to computing resources, such as cloud-based storage or virtual servers. Many businesses and individuals would rather pay to access resources over the Internet, when they need them, than own them outright.

At the outset, cloud computing was more buzz than substance. For a time, nearly every company I worked with sprinkled the word *cloud* liberally throughout their websites, whether or not it made sense. (One company asked me to "de-cloudify" its website after having gone too far.)

People who work in technology are prone to getting excited about the next big thing. Analyst group Gartner tracks technology trends in its Hype Cycle reports. Even if you don't subscribe to Gartner (yes, Gartner has a subscription model), you can find many Hype Cycle reports with Google searches.

Gartner Hype Cycles all follow the same basic pattern, with poetic names that remind me of *Pilgrim's Progress*: the "peak of inflated expectations" gives way to the "trough of disillusionment," beyond which lie enlightenment and productivity.

As recently as 2008, cloud computing was in the early, inflated expectations phase of Gartner's *Emerging Technologies* hype cycle—lots of talk, little real adoption. By 2011, cloud computing had its own Hype Cycle report. It went from an emerging technology to a *category of its own* in only three years.

Cloud computing has transcended the hype to transform the software industry, shifting market leadership and market share. As with many disruptive innovations, the existing players haven't gone away, but they've had to evolve or face significant competition from cloud-based entrants. Disrupted markets include:

- Email (Google Apps challenging Microsoft Exchange)
- Customer Relationship Management (Salesforce challenging Oracle Siebel and others)
- Storage (Dropbox, Box, and others disrupting on-premises storage)

Established vendors are responding by launching their own cloud-based solutions, acquiring cloud-based competitors, or transitioning their packaged software to service-based offerings.

More telling, most *new* revenues come from vendors offering cloud-based (or Software as a Service) applications. According to analyst firm IDC:[2]

- Cloud computing is growing at a compounded annual growth rate of more than 20 percent. That's double the growth rate for traditional technology models.
- More than 80 percent of new applications on the market are cloud-based.
- As businesses replace applications, many are turning to the cloud, with 34 percent of replacement spending going to cloud-based (SaaS) applications.

Cloud computing disruption also affects the hardware vendors. What happens to server sales when many start-ups choose to host their applications using public cloud infrastructure from Amazon or Google rather than buying servers? The cloud still runs on hardware, but *where* and *how* it is sold has changed.

Research firm IDC suggests that in most software businesses, growth is happening in recurring, subscription-based sales rather than packaged software sales. Revenues from software businesses without any subscription component are *shrinking* as a portion of overall software revenues.[3]

XaaS Drives Revenue Growth

How Does Cloud in the Portfolio Impact Revenue?

2012-2017 CAGR

- ■ SaaS/PaaS Revenue
- ■ Packaged Software Revenue
- ■ Revenue from companies with No SaaS/PaaS

Software subscriptions have the highest revenue growth.
(Source: IDC, 2014)

The writing is on the wall, at least for the software industry: for revenue growth, look to subscription-based offerings, not to traditional, "linear" sales models such as packaged software with perpetual licenses.

The Start-ups Are Coming!

Cloud computing and Software as a Service may be leading the subscription shift, but a growing number of start-ups in other industries are lining up behind them.

In the consumer market, any goods or services that people use regularly are tempting candidates for subscription-based start-ups.

Dollar Shave Club (DollarShaveClub.com) launched its personal grooming products subscription business with monthly deliveries of razor blades and hilarious videos. (As of this writing, the main Dollar Shave Club video has more than 16 million views on YouTube.)[4]

Dollar Shave Club features its irreverent videos on its home page.

Subscription offerings are popping up for all kinds of consumer products, including toothbrushes (GoodMouth. com), body care and diaper supplies (The Honest Company), pet supplies, and even cups of coffee in New York City (CUPS).

A host of start-ups are testing subscription models on parts of our lives that we didn't even know we needed. Here are a few of the more interesting ones I've found:

- **Cosmetic and beauty samples**: Want to stay on top of the latest in grooming and personal care? Birchbox delivers monthly boxes of samples, based on your gender and preferences. You can then purchase the items you like from them—the upsell is built right into the subscription.

- **Pet food and supplies**: Let's not leave pets out of the subscription economy. Petco sells pet food online as a subscription (repeat delivery). And if pet food is too mundane, BarkBox subscribers receive a monthly box of toys and goodies for their dogs.

- **Personal finance**: Personal finance software giant Intuit has gotten into the subscription model in a big way with QuickBooks Online and Mint. LearnVest goes further by adding people to the service. It combines consultations with financial planners with the tools to manage and track the plan, for a monthly fee (www.learnvest.com). For small businesses, Bench provides business accounting as a subscription service (www.bench.co).

- **Airline food**: Yes, you read that correctly—you can now enjoy airline food at home. Air Food One offers weekly subscriptions for airline meals, delivered to your home. It's only available in Germany as of this writing.

By the time you read this, some of these start-ups may be gone. (I'm not sure about the airline food idea, myself.) But for every subscription-based business that fails, another is ready to take its place. The subscription model gives start-ups the flexibility to figure out their target markets and value propositions through trial and error, working with relatively small sets of customers. (See the book *The Lean Startup* by Eric Reis for more information on this methodology.)

No Industry Is Immune From Business Model Changes

Subscription business models are emerging in long established industries, as well. Relatively stable business-to-business industries are developing new revenue streams through managed services, while *sharing economy* businesses shake up competitive consumer industries.

Managed Services

Established vendors in business-to-business markets are adding value and building recurring revenue streams through *managed services* models. A managed service combines equipment and services as a subscription solution. The managed service provider retains ownership of any equipment, and provides additional value to the customer by managing that equipment.

Printer manufacturers like Xerox and HP offer managed print services to their business clients. The packaged services include:

- Working with the business customer to scope printing needs (color, capacity, locations, etc.)
- Selecting the right locations for the various printers
- Installing and configuring the printers
- Stocking paper and toner cartridges
- Maintaining the printers as needed
- Reclaiming and replacing the printers as business needs change

The managed services model works well in industries beyond technology, including industrial chemicals. Do businesses actually need to *own* the chemicals they use, or might they simply lease the services provided by that chemical? Using chemical leasing (or *chemical management services*), chemical manufacturers and distributors work with industrial customers to determine the need, then supply and manage the appropriate chemicals for the job.

Chemical suppliers are compensated for the *effectiveness* of their chemicals, not the volumes they sell. From an environmental perspective, everyone benefits by doing critical processes with fewer chemicals. The service providers have the necessary knowledge to handle and dispose of the chemicals safely and responsibly.

Major U.S. and European manufacturers use chemical management services, including GM, Lockheed Martin, Harley Davidson, and Seagate. [5] The UN Industrial Development Organization (UNIDO) has promoted the concept for a decade. (Thanks to Ensia media for bringing this story to my attention.)

The Sharing Economy

Sharing economy businesses are making waves in established industries such as hospitality and transportation. Sharing economy businesses are built on the concept that people really want *access* to goods, not *ownership* of them. The model works particularly well for things you only need to access occasionally. Sharing economy businesses often rely on subscriptions and memberships.

Consider the typical car-sharing service. You sign up or subscribe to a service. Then you reserve a car when you need it and pick it up at the local lot. Zipcar offers plans with different combinations of monthly and hourly charges, inclusive of gas and insurance. It's a great deal for people in urban areas with only the occasional need for a car.

Are established businesses interested in this sharing thing? You bet. Avis bought Zipcar. U-Haul launched its own car-sharing service. BMW has an electric car-sharing service (DriveNow) using its electric vehicles. You pay a one-time fee to join and then pay as you use the cars. And Toyota is testing a car-sharing program using its three-wheeled, electric i-Road vehicles in Grenoble, France.

The sharing economy is large and growing. Jeremiah Owyang, founder of the Crowd Companies Council, suggests that since the model began in 2002, collaborative economy start-ups have raised nearly seven billion dollars in funding.[6]

> If you think your industry cannot be disrupted by the subscription economy, you're probably not thinking hard enough.

Other Trends Accelerating the Shift to Subscriptions

If you need additional evidence about the inevitability of the coming growth in subscriptions, consider how subscriptions participate in other major trends happening today.

Mobility: The simple mobile phone has become a powerful computing device, catering to our appetite for constant connectivity and instant gratification. (Some pundits call this the On-Demand Economy.) Many of today's start-ups use mobile apps, and many of those apps have a paid subscription component.

Internet of Things: The term *Internet of Things* (often abbreviated to IoT) refers to the growing number of devices with embedded Internet connectivity. For example, sensors in industrial equipment or health care monitors may monitor and transmit data to applications that aggregate and analyze it, feeding the Big Data trend.

> The Internet of Things opens up the possibility for vendors of devices to offer subscription-based services alongside the devices they sell.

In a world of networked devices and appliances, consumers maintain ongoing relationships with the vendors of their devices through mobile or web-based applications. Devices like smart thermostats (Nest), wearable fitness technologies (Fitbit and others), and solar panels all have their own apps. Today, vendors make most or all of their revenues from the sale of the device itself rather than the accompanying app. But the existence of this data creates opportunities for businesses to offer additional, subscription-based services using the data collected. They can also offer services to remotely manage groups of connected devices.

Fitbit provides its application and software for free when you purchase the device, but offers a premium subscription with extra reporting and analysis. This is one example of a *freemium* model, in which a majority of customers use a free service supported by the smaller number of customers who pay for premium capabilities.

Digitization: The digitization of consumer goods makes it easier to build subscription services around them. The music industry, for example, has seen shifts from physical media (CDs) to digital media (iTunes and MP3s) to streaming media services, in which you do not own the music at all. The move to online delivery made it possible to *subscribe* to music, either as a supplement to owning CDs or replacing ownership altogether.

Resource Scarcity: With more than seven billion people on the planet, there's no escaping the fact that we live in an age of increasing scarcity. Resource scarcity will inevitably result in price increases that will affect everyone.

As businesses adapt to a world of dwindling resources, they will need to work with their customers to reduce waste or reclaim resources.

As Andrew Winston writes in *The Big Pivot*,

> To make this kind of pivot and support billions of people with a good quality of life, ... we need heretical innovation in how business operates—creating processes that recapture valuable materials from products at the end of their useful lives—and toward business models that help reduce consumption.[7]

The *circular economy* refers to a model in which resources are reused and refurbished rather than mined and tossed into landfills. (To learn more about the circular economy, visit the Ellen MacArthur Foundation site.)

Carpet tile manufacturer Interface pioneered the idea of carpeting-as-a-service to close the loop on carpet manufacturing and recycling. Interface offers customers the option of leasing carpeting for commercial buildings, then reclaims and recycles the tiles when they are no longer needed. This business model significantly reduces the environmental footprint of the carpeting.

Dutch carpet manufacturer Desso also has a Cradle to Cradle practice, leasing carpet tiles and then reclaiming them to control the resources throughout the entire product life cycle. According to CEO Stef Kranendijk, in an interview with the Ellen MacArthur Foundation:

> The idea is to become a service industry, relying on a leasing system: then you don't buy the product, you only pay for its use, which means materials remain our responsibility and of course it's not our interest to see them wasted, at the end everybody wins.[8]

The circular economy is only possible if the company providing the product retains ownership within the context of a sustained relationship with its customers. Often, that ongoing relationship is a subscription.

Chapter 2:

Managing Multiple Business Models

The emergence of the subscription economy is not happening evenly across all industry segments and sectors, nor am I suggesting that subscriptions will *replace* other business models. However, subscriptions account for a growing percentage of revenues and deserve attention from a wide variety of businesses.

This chapter is for those of you working with businesses that started with other business models and are either exploring or making a shift to subscriptions. (If your business is entirely subscription-based, skip ahead to the next chapter.)

Many businesses start by adding a subscription business alongside existing packaged or linear sales models. Managing multiple business models can be awkward. A subscription sales model affects various parts of your business, including sales, finance, research and development, and customer success. The marketing organization must adapt as well. (The next chapter covers the marketing challenges in more detail.)

Established businesses adding subscription offerings tend to fit into one of the following patterns:

- The limited subscription trial
- The segmented subscription approach
- The "all-in" pivot
- The integrated subscription model

Each approach has its advantages and challenges.

The Limited Trial

Established companies seeing success with non-subscription business models may have little enthusiasm for making a transition to subscriptions.

Trial runs of subscription offerings face resistance from those who want to protect the current revenue stream. Advocates of subscription models must appease any subscription skeptics in their own business.

The most common approach for these businesses is to create a trial of a subscription model, to see if the market is interested. The basic premise is: "Let's put out a subscription-based version of our traditional offering and see if anyone buys it."

While a market trial is valuable, you should be aware of the following challenges that may doom your results.

Time frame: The successful adoption of a subscription model requires a longer-term perspective. In a traditional retail or packaged goods model, all the revenue comes up front, at the point of the sale. Subscription revenues are earned over time. A new subscription customer doesn't deliver a great deal of revenue in the first month or year. Revenues from a new subscription practice may look paltry compared with existing revenue streams for some time.

Inadequate commitment: A subscription trial requires a commitment of resources for a chance to succeed. When you are concerned about protecting the existing revenue streams from erosion through subscription sales, and don't take the extra steps to help customers realize value after the sale, you're not likely to achieve success.

A trial without sufficient commitment and resources behind it may flounder. Stagnant or small revenues from a subscription product confirm the skeptic's hypothesis that a subscription model doesn't fit the market. Failure becomes a self-fulfilling prophecy. You'll hear rationalizations like "Our buyers aren't interested in subscriptions" or "That doesn't work for what we do." Complacency can be dangerous in competitive markets.

The Segmented Subscription Approach

One way to manage multiple business models is to segment the audience that you're targeting with the subscription model, and then dedicate marketing and customer success efforts to that segment. This approach lets you develop targeted value propositions for different markets.

The segmented approach works well either on a trial basis or as an ongoing model. The challenges include allocating resources for the different business models and maintaining consistency across the entire business.

If the subscription segment represents a new market, then you have all the challenges of learning that new market segment. One enterprise software company I worked with made an unsuccessful attempt to launch a subscription version of their solution targeting smaller businesses. The dual learning curve proved too steep, so the business eventually acquired an established cloud-based business to add to their portfolio.

Acquiring a subscription-based solution presents the challenge of integrating two different marketing and sales organizations. In the software industry, you also have to address code integration.

Another business created an entirely separate product line, branding, and website for the cloud-based version of its software. This company recognized that the larger market opportunity was in the cloud-based business and put most of its weight behind those efforts. The packaged software became a secondary offering. The company sustained its existing customers, but put its marketing and sales focus behind the cloud solution.

At some point, you may have to decide which model will get most of your resources (development, marketing) going forward.

The "All-in" Pivot

If the subscription segment is particularly successful, you may choose to make the transition to a subscription-only model, either for a specific solution set or the entire business.

Adobe® Systems executed a subscription pivot for its Creative Suite® software. It started with parallel offerings, launching Creative Cloud® in October 2011 as a subscription, cloud-based version of its popular packaged design software. Adobe maintained both subscription (cloud) and packaged software versions of the products for more than a year.

In May 2013, the company announced that it would no longer develop new features for the packaged software, but would focus its development efforts exclusively on the cloud-based version. According to Adobe's press release, the decision was about accelerating innovation:

> Focusing development on Creative Cloud will not only accelerate the rate at which Adobe can innovate but also broaden the type of innovation the company can offer the creative community.[9]

A close reading of the materials provided to investors reveals that Adobe believes its future lies in subscriptions. In its investor presentations, the company stresses that the move to the cloud is about increasing business velocity and driving new customer acquisition.

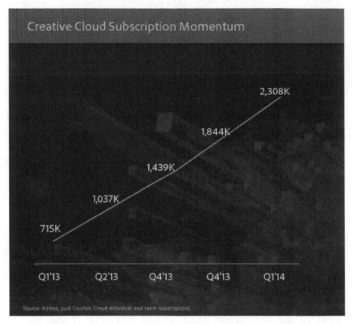

Creative Cloud subscriptions drive revenue growth for Adobe.

This all-in commitment has helped the company realize significant growth in subscriptions for Creative Cloud, while laying the groundwork for other cloud-based offerings, such as Adobe Marketing Cloud.[10]

The Integrated Subscription Model

In certain situations, the subscription model doesn't *threaten* existing business models—it supports and enhances them. Businesses may add subscriptions for the purpose of driving revenues to existing, non-subscription offerings.

As an example, consider the growing number of companies that offer subscriptions to monthly boxes of cosmetics and beauty supply samples. These businesses generate revenues not only from the subscriptions to the boxes, but also through further sales of the products in the box.

For a fascinating look at the world of subscription boxes, visit *My Subscription Addiction* (mysubscriptionaddiction.com). You'll find a huge range of categories of subscription boxes, including:

- Cosmetics
- Music-related gifts
- Candy
- Fitness/performance products
- Pet supplies
- Baby toys
- Wine, beer, coffee, tea

Online retailers are finding that adding a subscription capability can increase sales, even if they aren't committed to moving entirely to subscriptions. Companies like OrderGroove help retailers add subscription capabilities to their online sites.

According to Greg Alvo of OrderGroove,

> Across our 75+ retail clients—including brands such as Stumptown Coffee, Jockey, Kiehl's, and Zabar's—we've found that subscribers often have a lifetime value that is 200% to 400% higher than non-subscribers.[11]

Consider Amazon Prime, the subscription component to the massive online retailer's offerings. For $99 per year, the Amazon Prime membership includes free two-day shipping for eligible goods, free streaming of Prime Instant Video television and movie selections, Kindle book borrowing privileges, photo storage, and other benefits.

The Amazon 2013 Annual Report states that the company considers the costs associated with fulfilling Amazon Prime to be "effective worldwide marketing tools." The membership, in this case, is a way to market and promote doing business on Amazon. Win customers over with streaming popular TV shows and films and they'll jump on the free shipping to shop with you.

Balancing Multiple Models

When handling multiple business models, you'll face many challenges. For example:

- How do you sell subscriptions alongside another sales model? How do you compensate the salespeople? Who handles renewals?

- Do you recognize revenues when the customer makes a commitment or when they are earned?

- Is the solution messaging the same for both business models?

- Are you reaching a different part of the market with the subscription model? Is the customer profile the same?

- How do you price the subscription in a way that supports your long-term business growth?

If you're coming from an environment of marketing for the traditional business model—and particularly the enterprise IT sale—making the transition to subscription marketing can be difficult. Old ways of doing things don't work well. If you don't adjust to the differences, you may not experience the revenue growth you expect. The next chapter discusses the challenges that marketers need to consider.

Chapter 3:

The Marketing Impact

Marketing Beyond the Sale

For many years, marketing teams have focused on feeding the sales funnel. Whether delivering qualified leads to sales teams and channel partners or driving online conversions, marketing's prime objective is turning prospects into customers. Many companies even structure compensation so that marketing salaries or bonuses are based on lead generation or conversion.

When I worked at a start-up early in my career, lead generation was our all-consuming task. In desperate times, we'd resort to buying lists of leads from magazines or other sources. (I'm not proud of this.)

The VP of marketing characterized the relationship with sales as: "We catch 'em, you skin 'em." I hated the analogy, but it represented the state of the world quite well.

Today we live in more enlightened marketing times. Content marketing practitioners create useful content based on buyer personas. Keyword-rich content helps prospects find our content when researching online. We track and nurture leads through the sales cycle with the assistance of marketing automation solutions.

But the fundamental pressure remains to generate leads worthy of handing off to sales. In most cases, the marketing funnel stops with the acquisition of the customer.

> In the subscription economy, you're just getting started when someone becomes a customer.

A customer success management company called Totango conducts an annual survey of executives in Software as a Service (SaaS) companies. Many companies surveyed in the Totango Annual SaaS Metrics Survey were built from the ground up as subscription-based businesses, and rely on free trials or freemium models to drive revenues and customer acquisition.

Given their dependence on the installed base for driving revenue, you would think that these businesses would be deeply committed to nurturing and developing their customers. Yet even in this customer-dependent group, the survey reveals that the lion's share of focus and funding goes to new customer acquisition.[12]

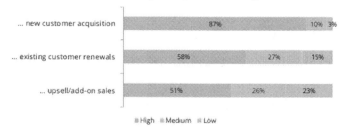

Data from the Totango Annual SaaS Metrics Survey, 2013

Supporting renewals from existing customers is *not* a high priority for more than 40 percent of the respondents. This is despite the fact that free trial and freemium models only work if customers using the free services realize value from them.

The survey revealed that many companies were *planning* to start tracking customer-centric metrics, including product usage and customer health. A full 49 percent planned to start tracking customer life-cycle value. Executives in SaaS businesses are starting to realign their marketing and sales practices with revenue realities.

The Revenue Implications of Subscriptions

Will that customer you just signed keep renewing for three years or more?

Subscription offerings have lower up-front prices than packaged or one-time sales because customers pay as they go. The longer a subscription customer remains a customer, the greater the lifetime value of that customer, even without accounting for cross-sell or upsell activities.

As you determine where to invest marketing resources, ask the following questions:

- What's the average cost of acquisition for a customer? How much does it cost to move a customer through the sales funnel, including marketing and sales activities?
- How long does it take the subscription customer to pay off that acquisition investment?
- What does it cost to maintain that customer over time?

When you account for the costs of acquisition and operations, a subscription customer is rarely profitable when they first sign up, even if they pay for a year up front. If you spend $100 to acquire a customer and they sign up for a service that charges $5 per month, then they must remain a paying customer for 20 months to recoup the cost of *acquisition*. That time frame doesn't include the operational costs of serving the customer.

Scout Analytics (now part of ServiceSource) examined data on acquisition and operational costs from various sources and determined that the average break-even point for most subscription software is 3.1 years. [13] Your mileage may vary.

The more successful you are at generating new leads, the more existing customers you eventually acquire. Ultimately, existing customers will account for most of your revenues, and will be essential to your profitability.

Companies that are building a new subscription practice tend to focus on earning the customer in the first place. But this is also the best time to establish practices for sustaining customer relationships going forward. Building and sustaining customer relationships requires participation from the marketing organization.

Consider aligning marketing spending and efforts with the *revenue opportunity* from existing customers, not just the revenue that customers are producing today. Calculate revenue potential based on how long you expect customers to remain customers and their potential for further sales. Chapter 11, *Building the Business Case for Value Nurturing*, discusses this topic in more detail.

Given the long-term revenue potential of customers in the subscription model, marketing must shift its focus past the point of the sale into the long-term customer relationship. As David Meerman Scott says in *The New Rules of Sales and Service*,

> You keep customers happy by doing exactly the same things that won them in the first place. You win customers by focusing on their needs. You keep them the same way.[14]

Chapter 4:

Rethinking the Funnel

The Traditional Funnel Stops at the Purchase

Marketing teams participate in many critical business processes, including positioning, messaging, branding, market research, competitive research, and other activities. But nearly every marketing organization feels the constant pressure from sales to feed the funnel—generating leads and turning leads into opportunities so that sales can turn opportunities into revenue.

Many marketing activities line up directly with phases of the sales funnel.

- Marketing activities that generate awareness (brand recognition) feed the top of the funnel.

- Once a prospect is aware of your company, the next step is to generate the lead, typically by collecting information in a registration form or at an event.

- As the prospect moves closer to a decision, marketing organizations deliver lead-nurturing content to help close the sale.

Most marketing organizations focus on the earlier stages of the funnel, with an emphasis on lead generation:

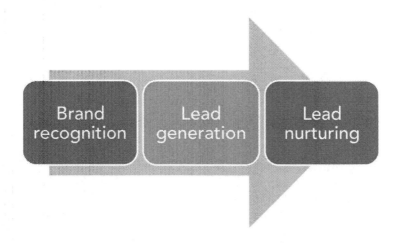

In the subscription economy, a growing percentage of your revenues come from existing customers. If you don't focus on existing customers, you're neglecting an important revenue opportunity.

> In the subscription economy, marketing's impact on revenue doesn't end at the point of sale.

Every marketing organization recognizes the importance of engaging with customers. We reach out to them for customer stories and testimonials. We hold conferences for customers and give their names to the press. But our processes and priorities are skewed toward brand recognition and lead generation. If you focus exclusively on the early part of the funnel, you'll neglect the critical, ongoing customer relationship.

The New Funnel Feeds Itself

If you accept that existing customers are critical to subscription revenue and business growth, then you also must accept that the initial sale is *not* the end point in the subscription economy. It's just a beginning.

You cannot abandon lead generation or nurturing efforts. But marketing's work is not done once the sale is made. You need to continue to nurture customers even after they subscribe, so that they remain customers, refer your business to others, and become highly targeted prospects for new offerings or versions of your solutions.

In the subscription economy, the sales funnel has significant feedback loops. It's no longer a linear, one-way path.

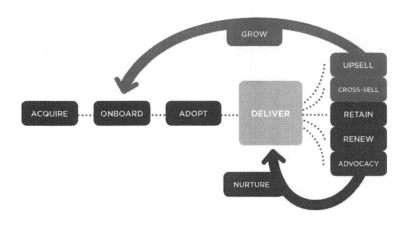

The subscription customer life cycle (ServiceSource)

Marketers need to add processes to support the circular funnel that feeds itself. The campaigns and processes in this phase wear many hats, including customer advocacy, retention, upselling, etc. We'll group all these activities under the broader term of customer value nurturing, or more simply, *value nurturing.*

Subscription marketing includes the following phases:

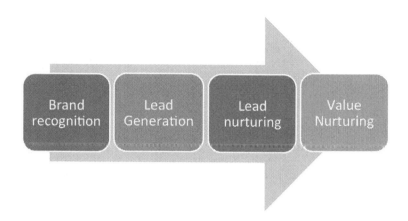

Every business that relies on subscriptions, memberships, and renewals should devote marketing resources and energy toward value nurturing activities. As you'll find in Part Two, a rich variety of activities and strategies can fill the function of nurturing value.

Chapter 5:

Value Nurturing

Nurturing Value in Customers

Beginning golfers are taught to work on their *entire* swing, including the follow-through. The follow-through on a golf swing helps to control where the ball goes once you hit it.

Value nurturing is like the follow-through for marketing and sales, ensuring that customers continue on the course you want them to travel.

Before the sale, you have to find prospects (lead generation) and convince them of the potential value they can get from your solution (lead nurturing). If you are successful, the prospect becomes a customer (conversion). In the subscription economy, the marketing responsibility extends beyond conversion to customer value nurturing.

> Customer value nurturing is the practice of helping the customer realize value from your solution.

The customer needs to achieve the functional or financial results they expected from becoming a customer. Marketing can help with that. Marketing can also help customers *recognize* the fact that they are being successful. Sometimes marketing can deliver value outside the solution, either in complementary offerings and services or in the business relationship with the customer.

Value nurturing turns customers into loyal or repeat customers, and successful customers into advocates.

Customer marketing is not a new idea, but it has been underserved in many marketing organizations. In the subscription economy, customers deserve renewed marketing attention. For that reason, I'm suggesting giving it a new label—*value nurturing*—that identifies the process as being of equal importance to lead generation and lead nurturing.

Many business activities already have value nurturing aspects:

- **Customer success management**: Today this term is associated with a function that lives either in support or sales, not in marketing.

- **Customer retention**: In practice, most customer retention efforts focus on finding customers at risk of leaving and convincing them to stay. The term typically applies to problem solving rather than creating value.

- **Upselling and cross-selling**: These are important results of successful value nurturing, but never mistake *selling* for creating value.

- **Customer engagement**: Customer engagement is one way to add value for customers. The broader issue is: what are you engaging your customers around?

- **Customer marketing**: Customer marketing is a broad term that covers a wide variety of activities.

Value nurturing as defined here is a specific set of activities, originating in the marketing organization, that take place after lead generation, lead nurturing, and customer conversion. It is the next logical step in subscription marketing.

The word *value* has inherent ambiguity that is useful in this particular case. Consider common uses of the word:

1. Value (*verb*): to consider something or someone as important or useful (Shakespeare: "I was too young that time to value her, but now I know her.")

2. Value (*noun*): a relative assessment of worth or importance ("What's the value of this painting?")

3. Value (*noun*): a principle or standard of behavior (Gandhi: "Your habits become your values, your values become your destiny.")

Value nurturing can help customers determine that the ongoing subscription is a smart economic decision (value in the sense of definition #1). Marketing can also nurture the customer's perception of the relative value (definition #2) of a subscription solution over time.

Last but not least, marketing may also help align the solution with the customer's personal values (definition #3). Some businesses use purpose-driven marketing to communicate and realize social or environmental objectives. Many people are interested in doing businesses with organizations that share their core values.

This third type of value, the alignment of principles or ideals, carries particular weight in the subscription economy because the customer maintains an ongoing relationship with the vendor.

Whose Value Is It, Anyway?

It's tempting to align value nurturing with monetary metrics such as customer lifetime value. How much money does the customer contribute to the business over the course of their relationship? How can you optimize that?

Revenue growth is of course your endgame. But if you approach value nurturing purely with the thought of getting more money from existing customers, you're likely to get it wrong. We've all experienced a poorly executed upsell at some point in our lives, and realize that it damages the customer relationship.

Your customers can tell when you're only interested in them for the money, not the relationship.

Value nurturing is about helping the *customer* realize value from your solution, not about helping you wring every dollar out of the customer. The better your business is at making its customers successful, the more successful your business will be over the long run.

> Revenue growth is the natural result of value nurturing done well.

The Five Facets of Value Nurturing

Just as the word *value* has several meanings, there are at least five distinct approaches to value nurturing.

1. Helping customers achieve their objectives using your solution (the traditional definition of "customer success")
2. Demonstrating value, or helping customers understand the value that they are getting from the solution
3. Adding value through activities beyond the solution
4. Creating additional value in the customer relationship
5. Aligning your business model and story with customer values

The chapters that follow share examples of companies that excel in one or more of these approaches to value nurturing. Depending on your business, you may find that certain categories or strategies are particularly compelling. There's no single formula for success.

If you market business-to-business solutions, make sure you read the consumer-based examples with care. You can learn a great deal by looking further afield than your own competition and keeping an open mind. In today's fast-changing marketing environment, stepping outside your comfort zone can yield results.

Not all the examples come from companies that are subscription-based. Nurturing one's customers is not unique to the subscription-based business. Consumer brands like Coca-Cola and rock stars like Lady Gaga alike recognize the value of maintaining audience loyalty. Subscription marketers can learn from many sources.

As you read the examples and strategies in Part Two, some may not make sense for your business. Identify a few that best fit your business and start with those.

Part Two:
Value Nurturing Strategies

Chapter 6:

Help Your Customers Be Successful

People subscribe to your solution for a reason. Maybe they believe it will save them money or make their lives easier. Perhaps it just seems fun. Whether for personal or business use, they expect some value in return for subscribing.

> The simplest and purest expression of value nurturing is to help your customers realize this value, fulfilling the implicit brand promise of your marketing.

The strategies in this section involve parts of the business beyond marketing. Smart marketing organizations in a subscription business are interested in all post-sale customer conversations. Many of these strategies align with *customer success management* efforts in the business.

Create a Customer Launch Plan

If you're looking for the low-hanging fruit of value nurturing strategies, you've found it. Creating a customer launch plan makes sense for almost any business and works equally well for subscription-based and traditional business models. There's almost no excuse *not* to have a new customer launch plan.

A launch plan helps customers start realizing the value from your solution as quickly as possible. In B2B marketing, we call it "accelerating return on investment (ROI)" or "reducing time-to-value."

The software industry uses the term *onboarding*. I dislike the term, and it doesn't make sense for all types of subscriptions, so I'm not using it in this book.

According to ServiceSource, provider of recurring revenue and customer success management solutions, if a customer doesn't start using your solution within 90 days, there's only a 10 percent chance they'll become a loyal customer. [15] Although this data may be skewed toward technology solutions, the general concept holds true for nearly all subscriptions. If people don't start using them, the reasons for subscribing in the first place may fade from memory. If it takes a few years for a subscription customer to become profitable, a customer that leaves early may cost you money.

Something motivated the person to become a customer. Marketing can help customers follow through and start achieving value before they lose momentum.

Technology makes it possible, in many cases, to see what your customers are doing with your solutions and spot if they're off to a good start or not. When operating at scale, find ways to automatically track usage and adoption. If it looks like the customer isn't getting started well, reach out and see if you can help.

- Your launch plan might start with a series of emails with links to videos or useful resources. Make sure to give people a way to opt out.

- For online solutions, embed tips and suggestions that show up the first few times someone logs in. Don't go overboard. Remember Clippy, the helpful paper clip in an earlier version of Microsoft Office? Poor Clippy inspired violent thoughts in Microsoft users worldwide. There's a fine line between being helpful and being annoying.

Don't neglect the power of personal contact. The more high-tech your solution, the more powerful a personal connection can be, through email, a phone call, or even a handwritten note.

Orchestrate an Early Success

The high-end restaurant business is built on repeat customers and customer referrals. A restaurant cannot succeed unless its customers value the experience.

Few high-end restaurants in America have the cachet of The French Laundry in Yountville, California. The restaurant has three Michelin stars and a waiting list measured in months.

The dining experience is fixed price (or *prix fixe*, since it's The *French* Laundry). Once a customer walks in the door, they have committed to the fixed price menu. And what does this famous, "impress your friends by saying you've eaten there" restaurant do? It hands you a tiny cone with smoked salmon and crème fraîche.

I haven't been to The French Laundry (*yet*, that is—I am an optimist) but I have heard the famed chef Thomas Keller talk about it.[16] According to Keller, every guest is offered one of these little cones when they arrive. Keller calls the salmon cornet "one of the most important parts of the meal."

The unexpected and whimsical appetizer serves two functions:

1. The gesture helps to relax a diner who may feel intimidated about entering this well-known dining mecca. What better way to break the ice than to give someone a treat that looks like an ice cream cone?
2. The appetizer launches the dining experience with familiar reference points. As Keller says, it tastes like something people have experienced before (salmon and sour cream), so they tend to like it.

From a marketing perspective, it's a customer launch plan wrapped neatly in a cracker: establish the relationship through a friendly gesture and create the first experience of success.

Use Videos to Accelerate Success

If your solution isn't intuitive to use, marketing should make it as painless as possible for new customers to get up to speed quickly. To meet the needs of customers with varying learning styles, provide instructions using different media. The more complex your solution, the more options you may want to offer.

In the business software world, customer relationship management (CRM) software doesn't earn its keep until the salespeople use it. And in general, people in the sales role would rather spend their time talking to prospects than learning software.

To speed customer success, cloud-based CRM provider Insightly delivers a rich variety of resources for new users, including:

- A Getting Started Guide delivered in PDF form (for those who still prefer to read)

- A link to register for a Getting Started webinar held every week (for those who do better with scheduled group instruction)

- A recording of the Getting Started webinar (for those who want to learn on their own time)

- A series of recorded webinars on various topics, including "Three Things to Do on Day One" and "Rolling Out Insightly in Your Company"

Video may be the best way to show customers how something is done. People can access it on their own schedule. Even for relatively easy-to-use solutions, video can answer questions quickly and help people over initial hurdles.

Zipcar has a series of short videos in which a Zipcar "co-pilot" talks people through the processes of getting a car, extending a reservation, fueling the car, and returning it. None is longer than a couple of minutes.

Help Customers Create New Habits

If your solution requires significant behavior change, you have the opportunity to help customers shape new habits. Guide them through the process of creating the habit, one step at a time.

As director of the Persuasive Technology Lab at Stanford University, B.J. Fogg researches how to use technology to change behavior. He suggests that lasting habit changes often start with small steps.[17] You can support these small steps using simple technologies within or around your solution.

Consider the case of Headspace, makers of an online meditation app. Meditation is like exercise; making the time to do it each day is a challenge. For Headspace customers to be successful with the application, they need to make a habit of meditating regularly.

Headspace eases potential customers into the meditation habit by offering a free meditation course of ten days, ten minutes each, or the "Take Ten" program. Once you subscribe for the free offering, the company sends a welcome letter with useful links and instructions, encouraging you to complete the ten days. At the conclusion, emails prompt you to continue with a paid subscription and more meditation courses. You can opt into meditation reminders, or ask to be connected with a meditation buddy.

Getting the reminders right is a delicate balance. As a business built to promote mindfulness and inner peace, the last thing the company wants to do is to irritate its subscribers. By guiding people through the start of a meditation practice and supplementing the software with reminders and social support, Headspace helps its customers build new habits.

Encourage Adoption With Gamification

Software makers rely on free trials to promote their offerings. But if people don't take advantage of the trial software, they cannot see the value of the solution. The more complex the solution, the more you need to motivate people to use the trial.

Autodesk®, maker of powerful 3D design software, faced this dilemma with its free trial software. The company decided to encourage adoption by adding a layer of gamification as part of the trial.

The *Oxford English Dictionary* defines gamification as:

> The application of typical elements of game playing (e.g., point scoring, competition with others, rules of play) to other areas of activity, typically as an online marketing technique to encourage engagement with a product or service.

Autodesk exchanged the usual software trial with an online game. In playing the game, Undiscovered Territory, contestants learned about the capabilities of the Autodesk 3ds Max 2013 software.

The gaming approach resulted in increased adoption, both of the trial and the paid software. By turning the trial into a game, the company realized:[18]

- 54 percent increase in trial usage

- 15 percent increase in people purchasing the software directly from the trial

From a value nurturing perspective, gamification can encourage customers to start using your solution quickly so they realize value.

Offer Great Training

In some situations, people need classroom instruction or hands-on training to learn to use a solution effectively. In the software world, administrators or power users may need intensive instruction or training, while everyone else can get by with a few videos.

Training programs represent a golden opportunity for marketing organizations to help customers get the greatest value from the solution. Because training requires an investment of time, it deepens the individual customer's commitment to your solution. If you do a terrific job of training, people are more likely to become loyal customers. And with massive open online courseware (MOOC), customers don't have to travel to classrooms to participate in training.

Amplify the impact of instruction by offering formal certification for those who go through in-depth training. Certification gives customers explicit evidence of their skills and makes the solution more valuable as part of their skillset. Many technology leaders offer certification training, including Apple, IBM, Google, Microsoft, Juniper Networks, Symantec, and countless others. Technology companies know that certified practitioners can become powerful advocates, particularly in industries in which people change jobs frequently.

Summary: Customer Success Strategies

The strategies in this section apply to nearly every business.

- A customer launch plan can be as simple as an email or video, or as complex as an online guided tour or personal services.

- If possible, track your customers' success in the early days of their subscription and create processes to keep them on track.

- Find a way to set customers up with an early success, even if it costs you something.

- If a successful subscription requires customers to form new habits, break the habit formation into smaller, achievable tasks and guide customers through those steps.

- Use videos to help people virtually when you cannot do so in person.

- Use gamification features such as badges, points, and online competitions to make adoption fun.

- Offer great training and instruction in the format that your customers want. Work with your training and education teams to make sure that the program delivers on the promises of your marketing. Offer certification when it makes sense to do so.

Chapter 7:

Demonstrate Value

Once customers start achieving success, marketing can discreetly remind them of the value they're realizing. The strategies in this section may be referred to as *customer marketing*, and range from sending gentle reminders to delivering personalized data. All share the aim of reinforcing the solution value in the customer's mind.

Share Customer Stories

Businesses love to use case studies or customer success stories as lead nurturing content, to help move prospects through the sales cycle. These stories are highly effective for value nurturing when you send them to your existing customers. (Thanks to John Morgan for suggesting this strategy.)

Although marketing organizations may ask existing customers to participate in case studies, we often forget about their interest in receiving them. Yet these stories are potent illustrations of how others have achieved success with your solution. The stories may remind customers of the benefits they are seeing, or inspire them to do more.

Most businesses already develop customer stories for lead generation purposes. Sending them to current customers takes little effort. Think of this strategy as a free trial of value nurturing, using content you already have at hand.

- When a customer first subscribes, send them relevant stories in their industry.
- When you release a new customer story, send it to existing customers.

This value nurturing campaign gives you an opportunity to start conversations with your customers. You may find customers using your solutions in different ways who are willing to share their own stories.

Quantify Your Value

The fastest way to convince someone that they're getting value from your solution is to do the math for them. If you can put a number on the value customers are achieving, share the good news with them.

Supermarkets use this technique regularly. When I check out at the local Safeway using my loyalty card, the cashier tells me how much I saved while handing me the receipt, addressing me by name. The transaction includes an immediate and personal assessment of the monetary value of subscribing to their loyalty program. (I pay for my subscription to this loyalty program with data, not money.)

If the value your solution delivers isn't monetary, you may need to be creative to put the data in context or make it interesting. For example, at the start of each year WordPress.com sends me a customized report about my blog, filled with statistics about posts and subscribers, and accompanying graphics and analogies. I could find the data on my analytics page, but this report is formatted and easy to share. It serves as a visible and attractive reminder of the cumulative effects of my blogging efforts.

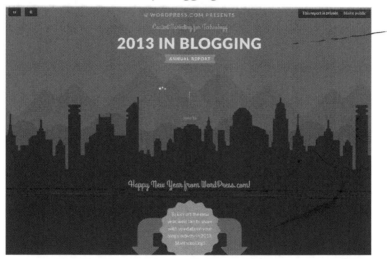

An example of a WordPress Year in Blogging report

Perhaps you cannot easily pull personalized data for each individual customer. Maybe your service is such that it seems intrusive to deliver personalized data. In these situations, try providing data aggregated across all your customers, without anything linked to specific individuals.

Aggregate cost savings or other benefits across the entire customer base and tell your customers about it. Sharing this information demonstrates value to current customers as well as prospective ones.

Summary: Demonstrating Value

Once a customer subscribes, explore ways to demonstrate value as they use the solution.

- Make sure customers see customer stories, videos, or other examples of how customers are finding success.

- If possible, put hard numbers on the value customers are realizing using reports, graphics, or dashboards.

- For value that isn't easily quantified, use analogies to put their usage or engagement in context.

- Aggregate data across your customer base if you cannot easily personalize data.

Chapter 8:

Add Value
To Your Solutions

Creative marketing organizations go beyond simply communicating the value they provide. They add value outside the product or service, through content, community, partnerships, and data.

Create Value Using Content

Try supplementing subscriptions with content that customers find useful. These offerings might include written materials (blogs, papers, ebooks, social media posts, books, and magazines), graphics (dashboards, infographics), videos, or other media.

As David Meerman Scott writes in *The New Rules of Sales and Service*,

> On the service side, once someone is signed up as a customer, information delivered at the right moment makes for a happy customer who renews existing services and buys more over time. And happy customers talk up companies on social networks.[19]

Using content to create value is a long-standing marketing strategy exemplified by businesses that use print magazines. AAA publishes a travel magazine (*Via*) as a complement to its insurance and roadside assistance offerings. Charles Schwab sends an investment magazine to its customers. For businesses with only occasional interactions with customers, adding a content subscription increases loyalty and reinforces value.

Print isn't dead, but the real growth is happening in online content. Many brands create online hubs combining written, graphic, and video content. These sites become legitimate destinations for customers looking for more than product information.

Birchbox provides its subscribers with a monthly box of personalized health and beauty product samples. To differentiate itself and add value, Birchbox also publishes an online magazine filled with articles and videos related to health and beauty. (*The Magazine* is the women's version. The men of Birchbox can visit *The Guide*.)

The visually appealing site includes articles that help customers get the most value from their subscription boxes. But the content goes beyond what's in the box. Interviews with authors appear alongside articles on how to keep your shift from coming untucked (spoiler: use tape), among other helpful tips.

If you adopt this strategy, the content you offer must have value on its own. This is *not* the place to pitch your product.

As another example, consider Adobe, a company I've already highlighted for its strong commitment to the subscription model. Adobe publishes an online magazine, CMO.com, for chief marketing officers and marketing professionals. (Since you're reading this book, you may already know about the site.)

Adobe editors curate useful articles and news about marketing and develop original content on trends and predictions. Adobe does not pitch Adobe Marketing Cloud on this site; rather, the company delivers valuable content for current customers as well as prospects. The content hub serves multiple marketing purposes, including brand awareness and value nurturing.

Don't want to do a lot of writing? Many people like to listen to podcasts while commuting or working out at the gym. Create a podcast series by interviewing people your customers find interesting. Podcasting has the benefit of putting a human voice to the brand. Business brands like Oracle and IBM use podcasting, as do consumer brands and media companies. Content Marketing Institute runs a terrific podcast series, *This Old Marketing*, in which Joe Pulizzi and Robert Rose discuss recent marketing topics.

Create Community

Connecting people in meaningful ways is an act of generosity. Businesses that make connections add value to their customers' lives.

Businesses are waking up to the power of building community in and around their solutions. Many software-based subscriptions build social features into the design, making community part of the inherent value of the product. Look no further than Salesforce and its Chatter function for an example of social networking capabilities embedded in enterprise software.

If you can't easily fit social features into the product, the marketing team can find ways to create community *outside* the solution.

Many businesses create and manage customer communities on social media sites like Facebook or LinkedIn. However, with everything else happening on those platforms, your business presence may get lost in the noise. Also, you need to collaborate with customer support or customer success teams to address any service issues on social networks promptly.

Some businesses go further by creating communities on their own sites (or "owned media"), connecting these sites with social media platforms as they grow.

American Express has always positioned its customers as *members,* implying a sense of community and inclusion. When pursuing small business customers, the company goes the extra mile by running its own virtual community, the OPEN Forum.

OPEN Forum gives American Express members a place to post questions and share information with other small businesses. Editors post selected articles on technology, leadership, marketing, and finance. The company calls it a forum for *exchanging* advice. This community adds inherent value to the American Express card membership.

In-person events often trump virtual reality. Salesforce is deeply committed to virtual communities, but it also hosts one of the largest in-person gatherings in the technology industry, the DreamForce conference. In 2014, more than 140,000 attendees registered, and millions more watched streaming video from the event.

Salesforce pulls out all the stops at these conferences. The 2014 lineup included famous musicians (Cake and Bruno Mars), politicians (Hillary Rodham Clinton), and inspirational speakers (Tony Robbins).

Why the big push around a physical conference for a company that prides itself on being entirely cloud-based? The in-person conference helps Salesforce build relationships with its customers and partners. It creates a sense of belonging and community on the part of its attendees. If the event didn't pay off, I doubt the company would continue to invest in hosting it each year.

If a business conference sounds too staid for your business, try emulating Red Bull.

Subscription companies can learn from creative consumer goods companies that live or die by repeat purchases and brand differentiation. As a consumer beverage company, Red Bull counts on people repeatedly making the decision to remain customers. Each additional purchase is a kind of subscription renewal. (The company also has a subscription magazine—the *Red Bulletin*—so you *can* actually subscribe to Red Bull.)

Many major brands compete for market share in the energy drink business. Red Bull makes loyal fans by connecting them with a community, both online and at sporting events. Visit the Events section on the Red Bull website, and you can find something happening on any weekend, in multiple locations around the world. Sample events include:

- Ski and snowboard "open jam" competitions
- Off-road racing and road rallies
- Ice cross downhill racing (this sounds crazy)
- Art fairs and music festivals

Red Bull sponsors and brands most of these events. Participants and observers alike become part of the Red Bull community merely by showing up. Customers meet and interact with other people who share their love of extreme sports. How's that for adding value?

Build an Ecosystem

Another way to add value to a subscription solution is to make it part of something larger through careful partnership selections. This strategy works well for brands targeting small businesses that don't have the time to select and manage multiple vendors. Each member of the network benefits from participating in the broader ecosystem.

ZenPayroll offers cloud-based payroll services for small businesses. The company built partnerships with dozens of online companies in related fields, such as personnel management and health insurance. By working together, smaller players effectively become a larger solution. Customers can pick and choose the applications they need, knowing that the various pieces work together.

Caveat: If you pursue this strategy, pay close attention to the quality of the partners you choose. Make sure you target similar customers and that the value propositions align.

Share Your Data for Extra Value

Many online businesses collect large volumes of data as part of doing business. That data may be valuable to your customers.

Netflix, for example, shows me a list of which movies are popular in my hometown. It doesn't cost them much to share this nugget of data with me. If I discover a movie or television show that I love through this feature, then that bit of insight increased the value of my Netflix subscription.

In another example, marketing automation provider Marketo launched the Marketo Institute to deliver insights from the data aggregated across its thousands of customers. Marketo will supplement the data with primary research conducted on behalf of its core customer base of marketing professionals. The company realizes the value of the data it collects in its network and is finding a way to distribute that value to its customers and prospects.

Summary: Value-Added Marketing

The strategies in this chapter offer a great deal of room for creativity. Choose the value-creating strategies that match your overall brand identity while meeting customer needs.

- Create and share useful or entertaining content through printed magazines, online sites, podcasts, or video series.
- Find ways to connect your customers in meaningful communities, either in-person or online.
- Develop partnerships that benefit your customers.
- Share data your customers find valuable.

Chapter 9:

Add Value to The Customer Relationship

Subscription success grows from long-term relationships with customers. Marketing organizations can take ownership of tending and nurturing those relationships.

Think of the strategies in this section as the "romantic advice" of customer marketing. Find ways to make your customers love doing business with you.

Overdeliver

Sometimes the best way to set the stage for a positive relationship is to pleasantly surprise the customer. In his book *To Sell Is Human*, Daniel Pink calls this concept "upserving."

Upserving means doing more for the other person than he expects or you initially intended, taking the extra steps that transform a mundane interaction into a memorable experience. This simple move—from upselling to upserving—has the obvious advantage of being the right thing to do. But it also carries the hidden advantage of being extraordinarily effective.[20]

Last holiday season, I used a service called Gift A Feast to send baskets of artisan foods from the San Francisco area to relatives across the country. (Lucky them!) A few weeks later, a box arrived at my door from Gift A Feast as a thank-you gesture for my business.

I did not expect the gift, nor would I look for it again. It was a delightful surprise, as well as an opportunity to sample the goods in person. (Yum.) Needless to say, I'm now a loyal fan. Had it been part of a "buy five, get one free" promotion, I wouldn't have had the same sense of delight or surprise. I was upserved.

Be Entertaining

Some brands are simply fun to do business with. I visit their websites or open their emails because I know I'm going to enjoy them.

Often, businesses use humor or entertainment as a way of getting attention from the world at large (brand awareness). One recent example is the Old Spice videos and "Smell Like a Man, Man" campaign. These videos exposed a mature brand to an entirely new demographic. More recently, GE produced a hilarious video for its new lighting using Jeff

Goldblum. And the most entertaining Super Bowl commercials often get more buzz than the game itself.

Being entertaining can help to sustain the long-term customer relationship. But being hilarious is easier said than done. You cannot predictably plan to have a campaign go viral. However, you can be fun and entertaining in your customer communications, like the flight attendants on a Southwest Airlines flight who communicate the safety features of the aircraft with humor. If you can't make people laugh, try to make them smile.

Be a Guide

Some brands help their customers feel empowered to take on greater challenges or do more.

Home improvement companies like Lowe's and Home Depot want customers to feel confident taking on do-it-yourself (DIY) tasks. Although not technically subscription companies, the stores count on customers returning again and again if they catch the DIY bug.

Lowe's balances humor and encouragement in its Vine video series. Vine is a platform for sharing six-second videos. The Lowe's "Fix in Six" series of videos offers clever solutions to common problems, such as unscrewing stripped screws, taking rust off knives, or removing pet fur from carpets.

The videos align with the store's brand objective of being the place to go to gear up for do-it-yourself projects. Customers can easily share the videos across social networks. (Find the videos at https://vine.co/Lowes.)

Lowe's integrates the *community building* strategy of the previous chapter by inviting viewers to contribute home improvement tips as a source for future videos.

Nurture Your Fans and Advocates

A customer advocate is a marketer's best friend. Loyal customer advocates feed the lead generation funnel by referring your business to others. They talk to press and analysts when asked and participate in customer testimonials, providing valuable credibility for your business. Advocate marketing programs help you nurture and develop those customers.

Given their value, use caution when soliciting advocates and customer referrals. In a rush to build a lengthy list of referrals, some businesses antagonize the people they most want to nurture.

Referral campaigns that attempt to make people *seem* like advocates can backfire. Facebook recently banned the practice of "like-gating" or requiring people to "Like" a business page to participate in a contest. A business that constantly pleads for likes and retweets looks desperate.

Offering money for referrals or advocacy can be tricky as well. If you stay current on behavioral psychology, you'll know that paying people for completing tasks (such as a referral) can actually *reduce* their motivation to act by replacing an intrinsic motivation with an extrinsic one. In a study by behavioral psychologist and author Dan Ariely, MIT students were paid varying fees to complete puzzles. Across different studies, he found that increasing the monetary compensation *decreased* performance for tasks requiring cognitive skills.[21]

However, sending an unexpected gift as a thank-you for a referral or story doesn't post the same danger. In the business or government context, make sure to check whether the recipient works for an organization with policies against accepting gifts.

Money is rarely the best way to reward brand advocates and referrers. Try giving customer advocates special treatment or access to events they find valuable and interesting.

GE does this brilliantly with its #GEInstawalk series of events. The company invites customer advocates and key Instagram influencers to private tours of GE facilities. Participants have toured facilities with wind turbines, jet engines, and heavy-haul locomotives. GE fans earn a chance to participate while the Instagram photographers share their experiences with the world at large.

Adding the social sharing aspect extends the reach of the program beyond customer advocates. Videos and photos of a #GEInstawalk tour of GE facilities in Fort Worth, Texas, earned thousands of Instagram likes on the same day the event took place.

Your customer outreach can be simpler. Don't underestimate the power of a personal expression of thanks. If a customer has said kind words on social media or referred someone else to your business, take the time to thank them personally.

Set aside the time to make personal connections with customer advocates, whether through a handwritten note, a follow-up call or visit, or other personalized gesture. As handwritten notes become rare, their personal impact grows.

Ask for Advice and Input

Have a new release coming out? Want guidance for a new campaign? Ask your customers for advice, whether for product direction or marketing messaging.

Many businesses invite customers to serve on advisory panels and solicit their opinions about new features or services. Not only do you benefit from the insight of your customers, but you'll also strengthen your relationship with people who enjoy being helpful.

The strategy works well for marketing campaigns, as Babson College has demonstrated with its multiyear campaign around the definition of entrepreneurship.

Babson positions itself as the educator for Entrepreneurship of All Kinds™, with business programs for undergraduates, graduate students, and executives. In 2012, the school reached out to its community and beyond to crowdsource definitions of entrepreneurship, collecting definitions on its own website (http://define.babson.edu).

The school kicked the campaign off using paid media to invite people to participate. Current and prospective students, faculty, politicians, business leaders, and alumni have all submitted definitions. The school has collected thousands of definitions, which it uses to create marketing and branding campaigns.

The Define Babson page invites visitors to submit definitions

Inviting community participation helped the school extend its reach beyond what it could otherwise influence with traditional, outbound marketing. The campaign has driven nearly two hundred thousand visitors to the Define Babson site, with unique visitors from 181 countries. According to Sarah Sykora, Chief Marketing Officer for Babson,

> We have been using our limited marketing dollars to engage our community and the market to share our message for us. Their reach is greater than our spending would allow, and third party sharing is much more powerful than us talking about ourselves.

The campaign served several purposes:

- It created awareness of the college among the broader population (lead generation). Sykora says that the school has seen an increase in inquiries about its entrepreneurship programs at all levels (undergraduate, graduate, and executive education).

- For prospective students, the campaign reinforced the school's commitment to entrepreneurship (lead nurturing).

- It infused existing staff and faculty with a sense of shared mission and pride (employee engagement).

- For alumni, the campaign forged a sense of community, potentially strengthening ties to the school (value nurturing).

That's a marketing quadruple play. The college has since expanded the campaign by inviting the global community to offer definitions of social innovation.

By welcoming and encouraging customer and community participation, you will strengthen the relationship of the customer with your business. As Simon Mainwaring says in his book *We First: How Brands and Consumers Use Social Media to Build a Better World:*

> The most effective way to attract consumers today is to invite them to share and help shape your brand narrative. Brands are finally starting to notice that loyal consumers want to be part of their brand's storytelling.[22]

Handle Breakups Gracefully

Even in the best of situations, customers sometimes leave. Let them go gracefully. They may come back if you handle the departure well. The marketing organization should write the end-of-life plan for customers, because leaving it to chance is risky.

We've all heard horror stories about people struggling to cancel subscriptions. Fears of an ugly breakup can prevent some prospects from subscribing in the first place. For an object lesson in how *not* to let people go, listen to Ryan Block's recording of an attempt to cancel high-speed Internet from Comcast, which you can listen to on SoundCloud (https://soundcloud.com/ryan-block-10/comcastic-service).

It's creepy to cling to a customer who's trying to leave. By all means, find out why they're leaving and try to address any problems they have. But then let them go with dignity. They might return. If they do, be ready to welcome them back.

Welcome Returning Customers

When happens when you resubscribe to a business you've left?

- The business might treat you like a new customer. You probably aren't insulted, but you do feel forgotten.

- You may be pleasantly surprised to find that the business welcomes you back. This approach acknowledges your past relationship.

- Some customer-centric businesses help you make up for lost time or pick up where you were before.

This third approach lets the customer know they were not forgotten, and may promote ongoing loyalty from intermittent customers.

If someone restarts a subscription, welcome them back like an old friend. Don't make them start at the beginning.

For example, create a welcome back campaign for resubscribers with content that varies based on how long they've been gone. Think about what returning subscribers need and find a way to help them achieve success quickly.

If you don't spend time around teenage boys, perhaps you haven't heard of Blizzard Entertainment, makers of the World of Warcraft®, Diablo®, and StarCraft® games. The World of Warcraft online game has between six and seven million subscribers.

Although Blizzard doesn't publish its demographics, teens and young adults undoubtedly account for a large number of its users. What happens when a dedicated gamer goes to college? Depending on the rigor of their schoolwork and the limits of their attention, many stop gaming during their college years. When they graduate, they often return to gaming, albeit with less intensity if they have demanding jobs.

Blizzard wants its customers to graduate from college and hold down jobs so they earn the disposable income necessary to resubscribe and extend the company's demographic past the age of 22. So Blizzard makes it easy to rejoin the gaming world if you've been gone for a while. When you leave, your account is frozen rather than deleted. If you sign up after an absence, the company connects you with resources that help you start having fun quickly, including

- A Returning Players Guide: The online guide includes account management, major game changes, new features, and the latest updates so returning players can find out what's happened in the online world in their absence.

- Incentives: Blizzard offers incentives to lure people back, such as a "Scroll of Resurrection" that rewards a returning player with a week of free playing time.

- Character level boosts: The company uses the occasion of new releases (expansions) in the online world to offer incentives for preordering. For example, a "level 90 boost" shortcuts the hard work of "leveling up" a character in the world.[25] These incentives help lure back inactive users.

These resources serve the purpose of getting the returning player engaged and playing as quickly as possible.

Summary: Customer Relationship Value

Use the examples from the businesses in this chapter to strengthen relationships with subscription customers:

- Upserve a loyal customer with an unexpected gesture or gift.

- Entertain your customers after the sale in your regular interactions with them. Become one of the businesses that they look forward to hearing from.

- Develop loyal customers into advocates for your business. Explore creative ways to reward customer advocates.

- Engage customers by asking for their advice and guidance, and then be open to hearing what they have to say.

- Develop and implement an end-of-life plan for departing customers, as well as a plan for welcoming subscribers who return after inactivity. Show them that you value their long-term relationship.

Chapter 10:

Help Customers Live Up to Their Values

Businesses that succeed in sharing their customers' values create strong, long-lasting bonds with their customers.

A growing number of companies are embracing the concept of the *triple bottom line*, which encompasses people, planet, and profits. New categories of businesses (B-corporations) build purpose into their cultures and structures. As businesses embrace social and environmental purposes, they earn a serious competitive advantage by aligning with customers' deeper values. As Simon Mainwaring says in his book *We First: How Brands and Consumers Use Social Media to Build a Better World:*

> The future of profit is purpose: Consumers want a better world, not just better widgets.

Customers are rewarding these shifts. According to the 2013 Cone Communications Social Impact Study:[24]

- Of American consumers surveyed, 54 percent had purchased a product associated with a cause in 2013.
- More than 90 percent of those surveyed want companies to support social or environmental causes, and 90 percent would be more loyal to those companies.

Customer loyalty is critical for the financial performance of a subscription-based business, so taking the high road can pay off over time. The following strategies require varying degrees of commitment. See if any of them make sense for your business.

Find Your Own Story and Values

Before sharing values with your customers, you must agree internally on your company values and story. Although the effort extends beyond the marketing department, marketing may take a leading role in spurring discussion and articulating the results in a compelling company story.

Values start with understanding your company story. Venture capitalist Ben Horowitz suggests that crafting the company story is essential to business strategy.

> The mistake people make is thinking the story is just about marketing. No, the story is the strategy. If you make your story better, you make the strategy better.[25]

Your story and your values are inextricably linked. What is the history and mission of your business? If the purpose and values aren't immediately clear to people inside and out, your first task is to identify shared values that the entire business can rally around.

The most powerful stories and values are closely aligned with the core business. For example, Dawn dishwashing liquid prides itself on cutting through grease in the kitchen sink. It's also effective at cutting through oil on marine mammals and sea birds. Dawn donates dishwashing liquid to the Marine Mammal Center and International Bird Rescue for cleaning wildlife affected by oil spills, and publishes videos of volunteers washing baby ducklings with Dawn dish soap. Who doesn't love baby ducklings? In the process of supporting an environmental cause, Dawn reinforces its brand identity and solution value.

In the business world, software giant SAP offered a free class on Sustainability and Business Innovation through its OpenSAP online training platform. The company's chief sustainability officer, Peter Graf, shared his experiences working within SAP, with its supply chain, and with customers to set and report on sustainability goals.

More than 14,000 people took the course worldwide. (A recorded version of the course is available on the OpenSAP site.)

In offering the course, SAP achieved two important objectives:

- The class helped SAP multiply the impact of its environmental and social sustainability efforts throughout its global customer base.
- SAP reinforced its role as a partner in innovation and supply chain accountability. Customers taking the course learned of the software vendor's commitment

as well as the capabilities of its software for managing the impact of their own supply chains.

Both Dawn and SAP chose campaigns that were aligned with their solutions and stories. Their values-based actions are tightly integrated with the brands themselves.

Commit to Your Values

Corporate values must extend far beyond the marketing organization. In the best-known, often-cited examples of values-based businesses, the commitment starts at the level of the CEO.

Under CEO Paul Polman, Unilever has built social impact and environmental sustainability into its core value propositions. The company sets aggressive goals as part of its "Sustainable Living Plan."

By 2020, Unilever proposes to "help more than a billion people take action to improve their health and well-being," along with halving the company's environmental footprint and enhancing the livelihood of millions of people.[26] It expects to accomplish all this without sacrificing growth.

The company reports annually on its progress toward these goals. This *isn't* a marketing campaign—it's a corporate strategy.

Many familiar household products are part of the Unilever family. Marketing organizations in those brands create campaigns that are consistent with the parent company's vision and story. Brand-specific campaigns aligned with the broader Sustainable Living Plan include:

- Dove's Real Beauty campaign, a long-standing campaign with videos, workshops, social media, and events designed to make women and girls feel confident in their beauty
- Lifebuoy sponsorship of Global Handwashing Day, a worldwide event that raises awareness of the role of handwashing in preventing the spread of many diseases
- Ben & Jerry Join Our Core Competition, a contest for young, socially-conscious entrepreneurs

Patagonia is another shining example of a business with values-based leadership. The founder, climber Yvon Chouinard, shaped the company's commitment to the environment. Patagonia makes headlines by encouraging its customers *not* to buy its new jackets unless they really need them. That's a truly revolutionary stance for a retailer.

Patagonia treats its customers like subscribers, prolonging the customer relationship to reduce its environmental impact.

- The company repairs items that customers bring in to the stores.
- It buys back and passes on used gear through its Worn Wear® program. This program also highlights the durability of Patagonia goods.
- Customers can return clothing and gear to the stores for recycling, keeping those materials out of landfills.
- Patagonia uses storytelling to shine a light into its supply chain efforts through its Footprint Chronicles®. Even before becoming a customer, you

can discover exactly where and how your jacket becomes a jacket.

Both Unilever and Patagonia are committed to a common purpose, from the CEO through marketing and operations. While CEO engagement is important, nearly every business can find ways to act on issues that its customers and employees alike care about.

Communicate Your Values with Customers

Once you have agreement on your business values and story, you need to communicate them effectively. Exactly how you do that will depend on your business' story and brand personality.

BarkBox has a simple story: a bunch of dog lovers express their love of dogs by creating a subscription service for dog treats. The company's self-declared mission is to make dogs happy.

On its "Frequently Arf'ed Questions" page, the company shares photos of its employees as children with their first pets. (Children and pets together are doubly cute.)

BarkBox donates 10 percent of its profits to animal shelters, rescue organizations, spay and neuter programs, and other dog-related nonprofits. It shares its values (love of dogs) with customers, and acts on those values in a way that is consistent with the company story.

Chipotle Mexican Grill aims to serve *food with integrity*, using processes that respect people, animals, and the environment. According to its website, the company's story is that it was founded with the idea that "food served fast did not have to be typical fast food."

The company created an imaginative animated video telling the story of a scarecrow encountering the world of industrialized food preparation. The theme of the video is "Cultivate a Better World." If you haven't seen it, search for "Chipotle Scarecrow" on YouTube. The video has received more than 13 million views on YouTube.

The Chipotle video was beautifully prepared, with high production values. Not every company has the budget to hire Fiona Apple to do music for a video. But we can all emulate the idea of expressing values through storytelling.

As Ann Handley says in her book *Everybody Writes*:

> At its heart, a compelling brand story is a kind of gift that gives your audience a way to connect with you as one person to another, and to view your business as what it is: a living, breathing entity run by real people offering real value.[27]

Invite Customers to Participate

Telling your story is a powerful strategy, but inviting customers to participate with you in that story takes value nurturing to the next level. Find ways to work together with customers in support of their higher values.

Online auction site eBay uses multiple strategies to collaborate with customers in meaningful ways. Using eBay Giving Works, customers can buy and sell products to support the causes they are passionate about.

eBay also invites participation around specific causes. In the aftermath of the devastating Typhoon Haiyan in the

Philippines, eBay launched a fundraising campaign, prompting people to add a donation to their purchases.

At the time, eBay was the parent company of PayPal. Its global reach and payment processing capabilities put eBay in a great position to make an impact. In the first 30 days after the typhoon, eBay and PayPal customers donated $23 million in typhoon aid.

Dick's Sporting Goods used a similar cause-related marketing strategy to support youth athletics in the U.S. A sporting goods business depends on people of all ages participating in athletic endeavors. Through its charitable foundation, the company created a Sports Matter campaign in early 2014 to raise awareness of the funding crisis in public school sports and help teams raise money for their operations.

The campaign included videos, social media, and celebrity endorsements. Dick's also sponsored an inspirational documentary, *We Could Be King*, about two rival Philadelphia high schools facing budget cuts.

The campaign helped 187 teams in 35 states raise the money they needed to operate. The Dick's Sporting Goods Foundation provided matching funds of $2 million, doubling the amount raised through local fundraising.

Do you wonder whether those fundraisers, team players, and parents are loyal fans of Dick's Sporting Goods now? I don't. I suspect that they will return to Dick's repeatedly, feeling positive about the purpose of the company.

In her book *Difference*, Bernadette Jiwa observes:

> Time and again the market proves that the value of stuff is finite, but the meaning we attach to stuff—the experiences we create around it and the stories we tell ourselves about it—has exponential value.[28]

Embed Values in Your Business Model

When it comes to aligning with customer values, the strongest positions belong to those companies that embed values in the business model itself. Values and business become inseparable.

Toms Shoes built its business with the vision of providing shoes to children in need around the world. According to the company story, Blake Mycoskie saw children in rural Argentina going barefoot and wanted to do something. He started Toms with the premise that for every pair of shoes sold, the company would donate a pair to children in need around the world.

Through the Toms One for One® model, the company has given more than 35 million pairs of shoes. Every customer participates directly in the company's story through the very act of being a customer.

Toms has extended the One for One model and product line:

- For every pair of sunglasses sold, the company donates eye exams and glasses to those in need.
- Toms couples coffee purchases with donations toward clean drinking water in the countries where the coffee beans were grown.

The company's mission and purpose enriches the value of the products they sell. As a customer, you don't simply buy shoes; you buy the knowledge that as you wear the shoes, a child elsewhere now has a pair of shoes to pull on. Your shoes suddenly feel much more valuable. Other companies have embraced similar models, including eyewear company Warby Parker.

What if you're working with an established business not built around this kind of mission? You can embed purpose into existing offerings. During flu season, Walgreens promotes its "Get a Shot. Give a Shot"® campaign. When a customer buys a vaccination at Walgreens, the company donates money to provide vaccines to children in developing countries, working through the United Nations Foundation.

Toms was built from the ground up with a purpose-driven model, but Walgreens was not. The Walgreens story is proof that you don't have to be a scrappy start-up to integrate purpose into the fabric of your business model.

In his book *True Story: How to Combine Story and Action to Transform Your Business,* Ty Montague suggests:

> People don't buy products; they take actions that help advance their own personal metastory, and sometimes buying and using your product is one of those actions.[29]

Caveats with Values-Based Marketing

The values-based marketing strategies described above can misfire if you aren't careful. Before you start down this road, beware of the ways that you can go astray.

First and foremost, you cannot fake your values.

The word *authenticity* is overused when it comes to social media, but being authentic is vital when using this strategy. The best marketing campaign will hurt you in the long run if your business isn't committed to the story and values you espouse.

In his book *The Big Pivot: Radically Practical Strategies for a Hotter, Scarcer, and More Open World*, Andrew S. Winston argues that with today's technologies and our interconnected world, businesses must realize that transparency, not secrecy, is the new normal. As Winston says, "The power of big data and transparency is a relentless tide."[30] If you don't align corporate behavior with stated values, eventually the world will catch on.

One of my favorite stories of radical transparency doesn't come from the world of business at all. The U.S. Supreme Court will sometimes edit opinions that they have already issued. This practice wreaks havoc for legal scholars that rely on the originally published opinions, only to discover that the law of the land is slightly different. The Supreme Court only sends records of these changes to a few paid subscription services.

To address this situation, V. David Zvenyach, counsel and part-time coder, created a simple application that crawls the Supreme Court website for changes and publishes them through a Twitter account (@SCOTUS_servo). All it took to bring transparency to the Supreme Court edits was a simple script and a Twitter account.

What does this mean from a business perspective?

Make sure your company story is legitimate. Remember BP's "Beyond Petroleum" campaign? BP's relatively minor alternative energy investments were overshadowed by the company's aggressive efforts pursuing oil reserves. Claiming environment values you do not embody leaves you open to accusations of greenwashing or hypocrisy.

> Make sure you have high-level buy-in for any values-based strategies you deploy.

Additionally, beware of relying too heavily on social or environmental virtue while ignoring other customer needs.

All things being equal, people want to do business with companies that share their values. This fact doesn't give you permission to ignore quality, functionality, or price. Whole Foods may sell organic food, but its customers don't sacrifice shopping experience or product quality. If you lead with environmental or societal value, it should enhance rather than replace the solution value.

Summary: Aligning Values

You don't have to change your business structure to take advantage of the strategies in this chapter, as the ideas here vary widely in difficulty and commitment. You might take a phased approach to embedding values and realize success at each step.

1. Start with finding your story and values. The more tightly the values link to the company story, the better.

2. Build the internal commitment to your values. It takes more than a marketing campaign to get your customers on board.

3. Communicate your values with customers through storytelling.

4. Invite customers to participate with you in support of their values through donations, social media communications, or other means.

5. Embed values into your business model, using purchasing models like buy-one-give-one or donating some percentage of purchases to a related cause.

Part Three:
Putting the
Strategies into Action

Chapter 11:

Building the Business Case for Value Nurturing

Overcoming Objections

Perhaps I've convinced you of the role of value nurturing and you see some strategies you'd like to try. Now it's up to you to convince the rest of your business. This chapter should give you the necessary ammunition.

Customer value nurturing is an *additional* marketing task, not a replacement for what you're doing already. You don't get to stop generating leads, building awareness, or doing any of the other tasks that drive revenues today. As a result, value nurturing may be a hard sell in marketing organizations already feeling pressured by competing demands.

Every good marketer knows they need to be ready to address sales objections. In that spirit, here are a few arguments to address the objections you might encounter.

Objection: "Our subscription offering is new, so we have to put all our resources into lead generation."

It's hard to argue with the importance of lead generation, especially for new subscription offerings. However, given the cumulative effect of customer churn on growth, the best time to start a value nurturing practice is at the beginning. With fewer customers, you have the opportunity to test and fine-tune your strategies going forward.

Start with a relatively low-effort strategy as a pilot project, then track its effectiveness. The steps you take in the early days will establish a culture in the marketing and sales organizations of serving the customers after the sale.

Objection: "Management wants to see subscriber growth, so we really need to focus on lead generation instead of customer marketing."

Remember that it's much less expensive to keep and develop existing customers than to acquire new ones. Reducing churn effectively boosts growth by ensuring that any new customers you do acquire aren't simply replacing ones that leave. Find more data below in the section "Customer Retention/Customer Churn."

Objection: "Our customers are happy. We don't want to bother them."

The "let sleeping dogs lie" approach to customer nurturing poses significant long-term risks. Your competitors aren't ignoring your customers—neither should you.

In a survey of enterprise IT decision makers and buyers, ServiceSource found that more than half of the respondents regularly received calls from their vendors' competitors. Even in enterprise IT, where changing vendors can be a huge hassle, buyers listen to the competitors who call:[31]

- 42 percent of the respondents accept calls from their vendors' competitors at least once per quarter.
- 69 percent participate in competitors' webcasts at least once a year, and more than 25 percent do so more than once per quarter.

As an incumbent, you have an advantage over competitors, particularly when switching costs are high. But if your key strategy for keeping current customers is hoping they cannot be bothered to change, then you've got long-term problems.

Besides, how do you *know* that your customers are happy? If you aren't engaging with them, you may be surprised when customers leave for competitors.

Objection: "What's the ROI? Is it worth our time?"

Ah, I thought you'd never ask. You can build a compelling case using metrics your business already tracks.

The Hard Numbers Behind Customer Value

The word *nurturing* sounds like something that only a liberal arts major would love. But you can justify it using revenue numbers.

If you need to build a case for value nurturing, find out if your business tracks any of the following metrics:

- Customer retention
- Customer (or revenue) churn rate
- Customer loyalty (Net Promoter Score or other measures)
- Customer lifetime value

Any of these metrics can supply the foundation for a value nurturing business case.

Customer Retention/Customer Churn

Customer retention and customer churn are two sides of the same coin. No matter which way you track them, value nurturing should have a major impact on churn and retention.

Because retention and churn compound over time, relatively small, incremental improvements can result in big revenue differences. Think of it like cumulative interest in a retirement account; small percentage changes make a big difference over time.

Assume that your annual customer retention rate is 85 percent and you have 1,000 customers. Without adding new customers, at the end of four years those 1,000 customers are down to about 522—just over half of what you started with.

If nurturing efforts improve customer retention to 90 percent (cutting annual churn from 15 to 10 percent), you'll have 656 of those original customers at the end of four years.

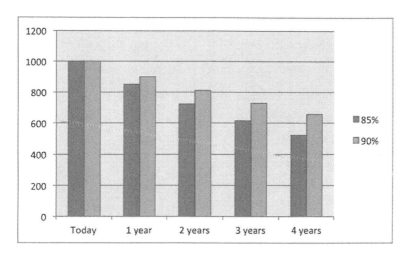

The difference between 85 and 90 percent retention

These numbers don't account for any customers you acquire in the interim. As your retention rate rises, more of the new customers represent *growth* rather than replacement. They become part of a higher baseline for the next year's customer retention rate.

New businesses may not worry about churn in their early days because making new sales to replace departing customers seems relatively easy. In a fast-growing start-up with $100,000 in annual revenue, replacing $10,000 lost to churn isn't a big problem. Your eyes are on the first million, not that $10,000.

The larger your business grows, the more difficult it becomes to find new customers to replace the ones that leave, simply because the numbers grow larger. When revenues reach $10 million annually, you would need to find a million dollars of new business to replace revenue lost to a 10 percent churn rate. That's just to stay even, not grow. And your investors want growth.

How can value nurturing change those equations?

- Effective value nurturing should reduce churn as more customers realize the value from their subscription.

- Value nurturing also creates a fertile environment for cross-selling and upselling. You may be able to expand revenues from existing customers enough to offset revenue losses due to churn.

Improving Customer Loyalty

Businesses use many tactics to measure customer loyalty, including monitoring behavior and conducting surveys.

The Net Promoter Score (NPS®) is one of the most common metrics for tracking loyalty.[32] This metric quantifies loyalty through customer responses to a single question: How likely is it that you would recommend [this company] to a friend or colleague?

Advocates of the Net Promoter Score claim correlation between the score and overall business performance and market valuations. Even without assigning a dollar value to NPS points, everyone would agree that customers who recommend your products or services are economic assets. Word-of-mouth marketing is basically free. Leads referred by existing customers cost you less to acquire than other leads and tend to convert more quickly.

A successful value nurturing program should improve the Net Promoter Score and other measures of customer loyalty or satisfaction. When customers realize the value they achieve through your subscription, they are more likely to recommend it to others. If you do a good job of demonstrating value to customers, they can share that information with others more easily.

As the NPS score highlights, the value of a loyal customer goes beyond retention.

- If you track NPS, you could use this score to prove the effectiveness of your value nurturing program.
- Otherwise, track the number of leads referred by existing customers. If the nurturing program increases lead referrals from existing customers, then you can demonstrate its value.

Increasing Customer Lifetime Value

How much is a customer worth in revenue to your business over time? What would happen to your subscription revenues if you increased average customer lifetime value by 5 or 10 percent?

The math behind customer lifetime value gets complex quickly if you dig into the details. But in general, a customer's lifetime value depends on three key variables:

Spending: How much the customer spends each period (monthly, yearly)

Margin: How much is left after the cost of serving that customer each period

Churn: The probability of the customer leaving

Effective customer value nurturing increases customer lifetime value in multiple ways:

- It reduces the likelihood of customers leaving early in the life cycle because it helps the customer achieve value from the solution. The subscription customer who repeatedly renews becomes more valuable over time.

- Customers who realize significant value from your solution are much more likely to either upgrade or extend their use (responding to upsell campaigns or offers). They are also more open to other subscription services you offer (cross-selling). Both of these behaviors increase spending.

Customer lifetime value is a predictive, forward-looking measure. While value nurturing should increase customer lifetime value, its initial effects will be visible in current or backward-looking metrics like retention and revenues per customer.

Changing the Discussion to Revenue Opportunity

One way to reframe the financial discussion around marketing priorities is to look at marketing spending in relationship to overall *revenue opportunity* rather than gross revenues.

Businesses are accustomed to the fact that they have to invest in marketing to generate revenues. Many align marketing investments with current revenues. The hundreds of companies surveyed in *The CMO Survey* spend on average between 8 and 9 percent of their revenues on marketing:

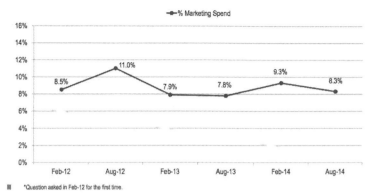

▓ *Question asked in Feb-12 for the first time.

Marketing Spending as a Percentage of Firm Revenues: The CMO Survey (August 2014), Figure 3.8, Highlights and Insights Report [33]

A subscription model requires a long-term perspective. A customer's potential value lies in the continued revenue you expect to receive if they remain a customer.

You could rightly argue that marketing should spend time and money on areas with significant revenue *potential* as opposed to current revenues.

The revenue potential of your existing customer base depends on:

- The subscription price paid by the customer
- The average length of time a customer remains a subscriber
- The customer's potential for churn (churn rate)
- The potential for expanded revenues (upsell and cross-sell rates)

The more mature your business, the larger the potential revenues from existing customers. Compared with new customers, these revenues have no up-front acquisition costs.

A small investment in customer value nurturing protects and increases potential revenues.

Chapter 12:

Starting a Value Nurturing Practice

Look Beyond the Marketing Team

Customer success requires participation from many groups, including billing/account setup, provisioning, consulting, training, shipping, and customer support. Product marketing and developers may be involved in driving sustained product quality for your subscription offerings.

In the subscription model, with its longer-term relationship with the customer, all these participants need to pull in the same direction.

Zuora describes its mission as helping businesses transition to the subscription economy. The company identifies the nine keys to subscription success by which it runs its own business. These keys include accounting and billing practices as well as nurturing and developing relationships.

PRICE

ITERATE

SCALE

THE 9 KEYS

ACQUIRE

MEASURE

BILL

SUBSCRIPTION SUCCESS

ACCOUNT

COLLECT

NURTURE

Zuora's nine keys to subscription success

Traditional marketing teams only participate in a few of these functions.

Organizational issues can prevent marketing from taking an active role in the post-sale customer interactions. A growing number of businesses are hiring "Customer Success Management" teams. (A quick search for "Customer Success Manager" on GlassDoor revealed more than 100,000 job listings as I write this.) These teams often report to sales, operations, or service departments and may claim ownership of the customer relationship and success.

Marketing organizations that want to implement a value nurturing strategy need to collaborate with customer success teams and others in various parts of the organization. While no single group owns the customer experience, everyone should take responsibility for it.

To collaborate effectively while nurturing customer value, you'll need:

- A clearly articulated description of what you're doing and why
- Cross-functional teams for implementing and tracking the strategy
- Agreement on metrics for determining the success of the strategy

Take Ownership of the Post-Sale Experience

The more groups involved in the post-sale process, the easier it is for the marketing team to step back and surrender responsibility for the customer relationship. And that's a lost opportunity.

Marketing plays an important role in setting customer expectations before the sale. Once someone subscribes, marketing should make sure that the business meets those expectations.

- Go through the customer setup process. For automated processes, make sure the user interface and design are consistent with the pre-sale experience.
- If you offer training, collaborate with the training organization to emphasize and promote the most important features.
- Set post-sale expectations appropriately. Create a video or quick guide so new customers know what to expect. Help customers find the features or

capabilities that you believe will deliver the most value.

Land and Expand

Many subscription businesses use free trials, the freemium model, or a "land and expand" sales strategy in which a sale to a small group primes the pump for a larger, enterprise sale. These growth strategies are built on the idea of achieving a small success and growing from there.

Use a similar strategy for value nurturing practices by running a pilot program and evaluating what happens when you start nurturing your customers.

Your first campaign serves as a study in shifting marketing focus to existing customers. Use this project to build cross-departmental participation, creating processes to track performance and learning what works. Start with a pilot program, then expand.

1. *Choose an easy, low-cost value nurturing project for your first campaign.*

Part Two describes a wide range of value nurturing strategies. Some work well with the tools and expertise you already have. Choose a strategy that fits easily into current marketing operations.

2. *Define what success looks like and how you will measure it.*

Identify specific metrics based on the selected campaign. For a training video, track how many customers click through to watch it and whether that changes their behavior. If you're building value through community, monitor customer engagement. While revenue growth and customer retention are your ultimate objectives, choose metrics that you can track immediately.

3. Test and learn from your pilot program.

Use the pilot program to test messages and learn which strategies are most effective for specific customer segments.

For example, if you're sending customer stories, try different formats (video, printed) and see which stories generate the most interest. If sending emails, use A/B testing of subject lines to discover which issues trigger a positive response from your customers.

Whatever you do, remain open to learning from your customers. You may find that customers have different concerns and issues from prospects.

Measure and Optimize Your Nurturing Strategies

Track the performance of your efforts during the pilot and beyond. As value nurturing competes with lead generation for marketing time and resources, you need to be able to demonstrate its effectiveness.

As with the pilot program, define what it means to be successful and determine how to measure your performance according to that definition. As you shift marketing focus beyond the initial sale, adopt corresponding metrics to measure your success.

If you made the business case for value nurturing using *revenue, retention,* or *customer loyalty* measures as described in the previous chapter, use related metrics to track your performance. These may include:

- Customer churn and/or revenue churn
- Revenue per user
- Customer lifetime value
- Customer satisfaction
- Customer loyalty

Many factors beyond marketing contribute to metrics like customer loyalty. Marketing efforts may take time to exercise a measurable impact on these numbers. You'll need to find more immediate ways to track the effectiveness of your marketing campaigns.

For example, you might track customer engagement with content, including:

- Blog comments
- Social media shares or mentions
- Click-throughs from email campaigns (to customers)
- Downloads of content or registration for online events

Marketing automation platforms can identify when existing customers engage with specific content on the website, without putting the content behind a registration gate.

You may also be able to correlate customer behavior with campaigns, such as:

- Increased usage of specific features
- Increased adoption (for example, increase in active users in a business)
- Referrals from current customers

Whatever your strategy, measure how it performs in relation to overall objectives.

Chapter 13:

Building On
What You Already Do

Which value nurturing strategies you choose will depend in part on your current marketing style and practices.

The modern marketing professional must be familiar with an overwhelming array of trends, tools, and strategies, including:

- Inbound marketing
- Mobile marketing
- Social media marketing
- Content marketing
- Search marketing

These aren't separate disciplines—they overlap. A few are essential tools for nearly everyone, the hammer and nails of your marketing toolbox. Others may fit better with some businesses than others.

Any investments you have already made in marketing technologies and approaches will influence which value nurturing strategies you deploy. Ultimately, the *customer* should be the guiding motivator behind your choice of strategies.

You can find marketing luminaries to help you with each of the topics above. (I've made a few suggestions in the "More Resources" section at the end of this book.) The rest of this chapter covers a few key tools and strategies that are relevant to the practice of value nurturing: content marketing, social media marketing, and marketing automation systems.

Content Marketing

Content marketing means more than simply marketing with content. The term *content marketing* has gotten so much hype in recent years that some people are confused about what it really means.

Content marketing requires a disciplined approach to creating content. You must first understand the following:

- Who are you trying to reach? Content marketers develop specific buyer personas to make the prospect very real.
- What are their specific needs and questions?
- Where do they seek help for those needs?

Then you create useful content that meets those needs at each point of their journey or relationship with you.

Here's Joe Pulizzi's definition from his book *Epic Content Marketing*:

> Content marketing is the marketing and business process for creating and distributing valuable and compelling content to attract, acquire, and engage a clearly defined and understood target audience—with the objective of driving profitable customer action.[34]

Note that the definition speaks of *profitable customer activity*, not just conversion. In the subscription economy, customer retention and development definitely fall into that category.

The largest differentiator between content marketing as a strategy and simply using content in marketing is *perspective*. Content marketing strategy is built around the perspective of the customer or prospect. Buyer personas help you understand the customer's needs and address them. You deliver content that educates, informs, or entertains. Content marketing is about creating content that your prospects want and need.

In practice, most content marketing focuses on generating leads. According to the 2015 B2B Content Marketing Trends report (by MarketingProfs and the Content Marketing Institute), most B2B content marketing goals are related to brand awareness and lead generation. A smaller number of practitioners use content for customer retention and evangelism.[35]

Organizational Goals for B2B Content Marketing

Brand Awareness	82%
Lead Generation	74%
Customer Acquisition	71%
Thought Leadership	68%
Engagement	64%
Customer Retention/Loyalty	57%
Website Traffic	57%
Lead Management/Nurturing	47%
Sales	45%

2015 B2B Content Marketing Trends report

Content marketing is the driving force behind several of the strategies in Part Two. If you have developed customer personas, then you're already thinking carefully about what your customers want and need. Helping them succeed isn't a stretch.

If you're already committed to content marketing, then value nurturing adds content and tasks to your objectives. Rather than focusing solely on supporting the sale, create content that helps customers achieve success or realize value through the solution, even after the initial sale. According to Joe Pulizzi once again:

> Goals to keep customers longer, happier, and/or spending more are the most noble content marketing objectives.[36]

Social Media Marketing

Most businesses have built social media presences on the "big three" platforms: LinkedIn, Facebook, and Twitter. Many post videos on YouTube, Vimeo, or other video sites. The "right" social network to use for business is the one where your customers spend time.

Several of the businesses profiled in Part Two use social media platforms beyond the big three, including

- GE's Instagram campaign for customer advocates
- Lowe's Vine video series

However, a social media presence isn't enough to build community. It's what you *do* with that presence that matters. The companies that experience the most success on social media run innovative campaigns and strategies that their customers find worthwhile.

Social media can help you extend the reach of your value nurturing efforts. For example, if your plan is to build communities through in-person events, social media networks expand the coverage and reach of those events.

Conversely, value nurturing strategies that originate on social media can easily spill over into other channels. Chapter 9, "Add Value to the Customer Relationship," describes Babson College and its "Define Entrepreneurship" campaign.

The campaign started by collecting definitions on a dedicated website (owned media). Contributors shared their definitions on social media, extending the reach of the campaign. The college received contributions from people around the world.

The school used those definitions to create traditional print ads in magazines, billboards, banners on light poles, and digital signs. Giant signs using the definitions appeared in the Boston, San Francisco, and San Jose airports—places that see many potential entrepreneurs passing through. The campaign spanned digital and traditional channels, and owned, paid, and social media.

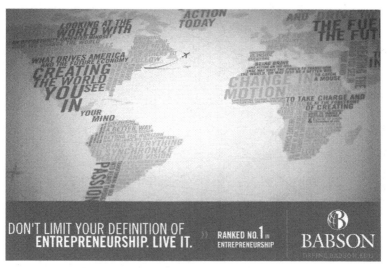

Airport signage from Babson's entrepreneurship campaign

Marketing Automation Systems

A marketing automation system streamlines value nurturing at scale. Marketing automation systems help marketing organizations by:

- Managing interactions with customers or prospects across channels
- Automating tasks and running timed campaigns
- Providing insight into what customers and prospects are doing

Many of the strategies suggested in this book benefit greatly from marketing automation technologies. For example, you could automate a customer launch plan using a drip email campaign starting at a fixed time after the moment of purchase.

A marketing automation platform does more than push messages out into the world. As a *customer engagement platform*, Marketo focuses on enabling productive dialogs rather than one-way marketing campaigns. According to Phil Fernandez, CEO of Marketo,

> No one is "automating" the market; what we're doing is scaling up personal interactions with the customer.[37]

Marketing automation tracks a customer's "digital body language" to provide insight into their state of mind. You can use this insight to trigger automated or personal interactions. For example, when a new customer spends an hour on a customer support forum, you might reach out personally and find out if there's a problem. By combining marketing automation with detailed online usage metrics, you can create highly targeted and personalized campaigns to help your customers achieve success.

Automation isn't the answer to everything, but it can free up time that you can use to make personal connections.

Don't rely on automated emails to support your most valuable customer advocates, for example. A human connection almost always trumps an automated one.

Chapter 14:

Four Fundamental Rules of Value Nurturing

In subscription business models, getting the initial sale isn't the end objective of marketing anymore. To continue engaging with customers after the sale, you need to abide by a few basic rules:

1. Be empathetic with the customer
2. Show your personality
3. Handle mistakes with grace
4. Don't be creepy

These guidelines aren't unique to value nurturing. You probably practice most or all of them today. But in the subscription economy, in which you maintain an ongoing relationship with the customer, these practices assume particular importance.

Rule #1: Be Empathetic

Run a quick litmus test on every value nurturing campaign: Is it about you or about the customer?

> Value nurturing should always start with the customer's perspective.

To find long-term success, your business must meet your customers' needs. A clever video that wins awards and goes viral is meaningless from a value nurturing perspective unless your customers find it valuable.

Particularly in business-to-business industries, marketing organizations often spend their budgets communicating how great their solutions are rather than how they help customers on their own missions. Some technology enthusiasts cannot differentiate between a product feature and its benefit to the customer.

Big brands are accustomed to being the heroes of their own stories. I've heard this request: "We need an article about how visionary our CEO is—let's make it all about him." Sometimes you have to cater to stakeholders other than the customer. But don't confuse this with creating content that your customers want and need.

Value nurturing puts the customer at the center of the story.

In the book *Winning the Story Wars*, Jonah Sachs writes about the long history of "inadequacy marketing," or marketing based on the idea that prospects *lack* something that can only be fixed with a purchase.

Inadequacy stories encourage immature emotions like greed, vanity, and insecurity by telling us that we are somehow incomplete. These stories then offer to remove the discomfort of those emotions with a simple purchase or association with a brand.[38]

With inadequacy marketing, the hero of every story is the product or service, or the brand providing it. We are surrounded by inadequacy marketing messages that we can be smarter, richer, cooler, or less thirsty if we simply buy the right products.

Sachs contrasts this approach with what he calls "empowerment marketing," or marketing in a way that helps customers on their own paths to growth or maturity. When you practice empowerment marketing, the customer is the hero of the stories you tell. Your solution fills one of many possible roles in the customer's journey and is an important part of the story.

Consider Apple's advertisements that show people doing wonderful or creative things with the iPad. In the 2014 holiday season, an Apple ad showed a young woman creating a musical gift for her grandmother. The device is the enabler, while the people (Apple customers) are the stars of their own stories.

Inadequacy marketing doesn't work well once someone has become your subscription customer. If your solution doesn't address a genuine need rather than a manufactured inadequacy, the customer will catch on and stop subscribing.

Value nurturing is all about helping the customer succeed on their journey. If your solution empowers the customer to be successful, then your business will also succeed.

Rule #2: Show Your Personality

We expect a lot from the organizations we do business with.

On one hand, we understand that every business is a collection of people. As customers, we want to interact with real people when we have a problem or question. Employees may blog or tweet in their own names, and company *About Us* web pages show photos and profile employees to humanize the business.

On the other hand, we expect consistency across all parts of a business. Whether in a sales or service interaction, we don't want to repeat ourselves, or get mixed messages. In this sense, we see businesses as single entities.

Our expectations for both consistency and humanity have implications for marketing in the subscription economy. Marketing messages, tone, and style create expectations for interactions beyond the sale. Marketing defines the personality for the overall brand, and the rest of the business must live up to it.

Whatever personality you express, it needs to be consistent with your business and the people in it. If you cast your business as a caring, value-driven organization, then you must behave that way when you interact with customers in all parts of the business.

Personality matters, even in business-to-business companies. Cloud-based enterprise content collaboration company Box does a great job of projecting a fun style in the enterprise software market. It helps that the company's CEO, Aaron Levie, is youthful, bright, and entertaining. The company works to maintain a consistent tone and style across all customer communications.

One way to ensure consistency is to create a brand style guide and share it throughout the company, *beyond* the marketing organization.

Tone and style extend beyond your written communications. They should apply to online interactions, phone conversations, and website pages. For example, if you click a broken link on the IBM website, you receive a polite and helpful error page, headlined "Our apologies…" complete with links for suggested actions and assistance. It's a great fit for a company that wants to be a trusted business and technology advisor.

In contrast, the Geek Squad is a technical support business built on a sense of fun. Its tagline is "Serving the Public, Policing Technology and Protecting the World." Employees carry "Special Agent" badges and drive GeekMobile® vehicles to customer sites.

Should you reach the error page on the GeekSquad website, you'll find a page with the headline "OMG! YOU BROKE THE INTERWEBS!" The page continues: "Quick! Click one of the working links before the fabric of space and time begins to unravel. Oh, and sorry for the inconvenience."

If you have a similar problem on the Lego site, the "Page not found" page fits the brand style beautifully, without a single word. (Try it yourself: http://www.lego.com/error.)

In each case, the expression of the brand personality flows all the way to the error page. That brings us to the next rule: handle mistakes well.

Rule #3: Handle Your Mistakes with Grace

In business as in life itself, when you make a mistake, own up to it and make it right.

When you engage honestly with your customers, you sometimes get negative feedback that isn't fun to hear. It's a golden opportunity. For every customer with a genuine problem, assume that dozens of others feel the same pain but say nothing. By finding and addressing the pain points, you can make things better for many customers. Be grateful to complaining customers, because they're giving you the insight to improve.

When you hear about a problem or make a mistake, it's best to deal with it quickly and openly. Social media channels magnify any mistakes, but if you deal with them openly, they disappear eventually. Try to cover up or blame the customer, however, and you'll reach a whole new level of negative exposure.

In today's highly transparent world, nothing makes your brand look worse than picking a fight with a customer.

One historic hotel in New York City fined its wedding customers $500 if anyone involved with the wedding wrote a negative online review. That's a terrible idea for many reasons, and it blew up on social media. (Moral of the story for consumers: if you're booking a wedding venue, read the contract before you sign.)

Rule #4: Don't Be Creepy

When it comes to engaging with current customers, look for the line dividing personalized from "Big Brother" and creepy. Don't cross that line.

Technology and "big data" deliver real-time insight into customers' online behavior. If you use this insight to create highly targeted campaigns that delight customers, that's good. But if you stalk your customers online and interrupt them with messages that demonstrate that that you're watching their behavior, that can be creepy.

Here's the problem: what delights one customer might distress another. Make sure you understand your customers. Where possible, offer people a chance to opt out if they find it intrusive. This is particularly true if someone visits your website and believes they are anonymous (they haven't logged in). Be careful about what you communicate with them unless you've explicitly asked permission to give them a cookie or leave them logged on. No one wants to do business with Big Brother.

If you're not sure whether a new campaign or idea goes too far, test it with several customers and see if you're hitting their creep factor. What matters is what *they* think, not what you think. As an added bonus, asking advice is a customer nurturing strategy. You may strengthen the customer relationship because you asked.

Chapter 15:

The Marketing Opportunity

All the strategies in this book are based on a central truth: subscription-based businesses have to maintain ongoing relationships with their customers far beyond the initial sign-up. Customer marketing isn't a "nice-to-have" function anymore—it's essential.

For marketers, the challenges of adapting to the subscription economy are many. I'd argue that there's never been a better time to be in marketing if you want a chance to make a difference in your business. As a marketing professional, you have license be creative. You can expand the role of marketing, finding ways to create new value for your business and its customers.

Creativity Needed

When the old rules of marketing don't apply, you have permission to make up new ones. When it comes to marketing for the subscription economy, everyone is learning on the job, and nobody has all the answers—even the marketing gurus.

Big budgets are nice but not necessary. Marketing powerhouses like Coca-Cola and Procter & Gamble are well matched by smaller businesses that understand their markets intimately. Content marketing, social media, and digital marketing level the playing field. In the subscription economy, changing business models are creating new platforms for delivering value.

Creativity is at a premium when storytelling is the new marketing imperative. As the examples in Part Two illustrate, people who look beyond the usual ways of doing things can make a huge impact with their customers. And happy subscription customers deliver revenue growth over time. As marketer and improv artist Kathy Klotz Guest says, "Safe is the new risky."[39]

Filling Bigger Shoes

Marketing has the opportunity to play a larger role than ever before in the subscription economy. To step up to this challenge, marketing organizations need to collaborate closely with all parts of the business involved in maintaining the customer relationship.

Many of the examples in this book extend beyond the marketing organization. The usual suspects involved in customer success include customer support and renewal sales or account management teams. You may also need to work with product designers, training and documentation, operations staff, and others to set and execute on customer expectations.

You may need to work outside your comfort zone as an advocate for customer value.

Increasing Business Value

Marketing is no longer just about getting to the sale. To keep subscription customers renewing and reengaging, you have to provide genuine value and solve their problems. This requires a deep understanding of the customer.

A growing number of people want to understand the values of the organizations that they do business with. According to the 2013 Cone Communications Social Impact Study, only 7 percent of Americans feel that businesses exist solely to make money for shareholders. And 25 percent believe they can have an impact on societal and environmental issues through their purchases. In other words, your customers expect more than just a business transaction.[40]

The need to strengthen ongoing relationships with customers makes it critical for businesses to understand and claim their *own* values. The good news is that employees are more engaged at value-driven companies. You might have more fun at work.

Marketers are in a unique position to help businesses shift strategies, focus on customer success, and make substantive changes as they embody their stories and values. Let's make a marketing shift and see what happens.

Join the Subscription Marketing Group

Interested in joining an ongoing discussion about subscription marketing? Sign up for the Subscription Marketing group from this book's website at SubscriptionMarketingBook.com. You'll receive new resources and examples. And I'd love to hear what you think.

More Resources

If you're looking for good books to help you with the strategies in this book, here are a few of my favorites.

Brand Against the Machine, by John Morgan (Wiley). This book is a compelling discussion of the realities of branding in today's world. It's full of actionable insight, and aligns well with value nurturing objectives of building a customer-focused brand and earning customer trust.

Branding Basics for Small Businesses, by Maria Ross (NorLights Press). I read the book after hearing Maria talk. Despite the title, her no-nonsense approach to branding makes sense for businesses of all sizes. She offers great advice about true brand consistency.

The Difference: The One Page Method for Reimagining Your Business and Reinventing Your Marketing, by Bernadette Jiwa (The Story Of Telling Press). This book is a fast but inspiring read, calling us to create a real difference in customers' lives.

Epic Content Marketing, by Joe Pulizzi (McGraw-Hill Education). Pulizzi compiles everything you might need to know about content marketing in one place. It's the modern content marketer's definitive source.

Everybody Writes: Your Go-To Guide for Creating Ridiculously Good Content, by Ann Handley (Wiley). I love Ann Handley's writing—here's your chance to find out why it's so good. This book offers insight into how to make marketing writing both fun and personable. Even if you're an expert writer, you'll find much to love in this book.

The New Rules of Sales and Service, by David Meerman Scott (Wiley). David Meerman Scott redefined marketing several years ago, with his *New Rules of Marketing and PR.* In this new book, he highlights the challenges of ongoing customer engagement. The topic is highly relevant for a marketer in a subscription-based business, as the divisions between marketing, sales, and service are shrinking.

Thinking Fast and Slow, by Daniel Kahneman (Farrar, Straus and Giroux). He may have won the Nobel Prize for Economics, but marketers everywhere should offer up thanks to Kahneman for explaining our irrational (and lazy) thought systems. To empathize with your customers, it helps to understand how they're thinking. This book reveals the vagaries of human decisions and thoughts.

To Sell Is Human, by Daniel Pink (Riverhead Books). This book is less about sales and more about human nature, empathy, and persuasion. It's an entertaining read filled with useful insight.

True Story: How to Combine Story and Action to Transform Your Business, by Ty Montague (Harvard Business Review Press). This book insists that brands must go beyond storytelling to story*doing.* Montague describes how an authentic corporate metastory transcends marketing and informs business actions.

Winning the Story Wars, by Jonah Sachs (Harvard Business Review Press). This book elevates marketing to another level, calling on Joseph Campbell's hero's journey, cultural myths, and Maslow's hierarchy of needs. Sachs's call for an end to "inadequacy" marketing and a new, empowering approach to marketing is inspiring.

Acknowledgments

My name may be on the cover, but the ideas and content in this book are products of interactions with clients I've worked with, companies I do business with, plus authors, speakers, and bloggers—too many people to name them all.

I'm particularly grateful to all my clients over the years, from whom I have learned through collaboration. The authors quoted and mentioned in this book have likewise been a source of inspiration, as well as encouragement and support.

If you want to affirm your faith in fellow man, try writing a book. Although writing seems like a solitary pursuit, you'll be bolstered by the support and helpfulness of others around you. This has been true for me. The process of reaching out and connecting with people about the book has been rewarding, and I am indebted to the generosity of many.

When it comes to gathering the detailed content for the examples and illustrations, I owe thanks to many sources. MarketingProfs, Cone Communications, The CMO Survey, Edelman Research, and Totango have given me access to research that enriches the content. Amy Konary at IDC helped me track down sources for their research.

Thanks to Carolyn Hotchkiss for telling me about Babson's Define campaign, and to Sarah Sykora for sharing detailed information about the school's objectives and results from the campaign.

At ServiceSource, particular thanks go to Randy Brasche, Jim Dunham, and everyone who has shared with me their expertise on recurring revenues.

The publishing process itself has benefitted from the efforts and help of many individuals. I'm grateful for Holly Brady's guidance and Thomas McGee's brilliant cover design. Amy Garvey and Mark Rhynsburger have improved the text with their editorial acumen.

Ongoing encouragement, support, and feedback have been welcome from many people, including Lisa Abbott, Christopher Bartik, Lincoln Murphy, Kaiser Mulla-Feroze, Tracey Sestilli, Ann Handley, Joe Pulizzi, David Meerman Scott, Kathy Klotz Guest, John Morgan, John Robb, Tom Hogan, and Carol Broadbent.

The wise members of Women in Consulting have been an ongoing source of inspiration and support. Whether she knows it or not, Kate Purmal helped to set me on this path.

And my family has been endlessly patient and supportive through the entire process. They have brought me examples of subscription successes, found errors, and made suggestions to make the book better. I am forever grateful for their love and support.

Notes

[1] "2014 Edelman Trust Barometer, Trust in Business," http://www.edelman.com/insights/intellectual-property/2014-edelman-trust-barometer/trust-in-business.

[2] IDC, 2014.

[3] IDC, 2014.

[4] "DollarShaveClub.com: Our Blades are F***ing Great," YouTube video, https://www.youtube.com/watch?v=ZUG9qYTJMsI.

[5] Elizabeth Grossman, "Cleaning Up with Rent-A-Chemical," Ensia Media, September 15, 2014, http://ensia.com/features/cleaning-up-with-rent-a-chemical.

[6] Jeremiah Owyang, "Funding Comparison: Collaborative Economy Rivals Popular Social Network Funding," on the *Web Strategist* blog, November 14, 2014, http://www.web-strategist.com/blog/2014/11/14/funding-comparison-social-networks-and-collaborative-economy.

[7] Andrew S. Winston, *The Big Pivot*, Harvard Business Review Press (2014), p. 46.

[8] "Desso, 10 Years to Close the Loop," a case study by The Ellen MacArthur Foundation, http://www.ellenmacarthurfoundation.org/business/articles/desso-10-years-to-close-the-loop.

[9] "Adobe Accelerates Shift to the Cloud," Adobe Press Release, May 6, 2013.

[10] Adobe Investor Handout, July 2014, http://wwwimages.adobe.com/content/dam/Adobe/en/investor-relations/PDFs/ADBE-Investor-Handout-July-2014.pdf.

[11] Greg Alvo, "The Case for Subscription Commerce and 5 Tips for Successful Implementation," FastCompany, February 26, 2014.

[12] "2013 Totango Annual SaaS Metrics Survey," http://www.totango.com/resources/2013-totango-annual-saas-metrics-survey

[13] Matt Shanahan, "Why You Need to Know The Lifetime Value of Customer Relationships," Scout Analytics blog (ServiceSource), http://research.scoutanalytics.com/revenue-retention/why-you-need-to-know-the-lifetime-value-of-customer-relationships.

[14] David Meerman Scott, *The New Rules of Sales and Service: How to Use Agile Selling, Real-Time Customer Engagement, Big Data, Content, and Storytelling to Grow Your Business*, Wiley (2014), p 169.

[15] ServiceSource customer research, 2014, http://research.scoutanalytics.com/churn/the-9010-rule-of-adoption-and-customer-success/

[16] Thomas Keller was a guest on NPR's radio show *Wait Wait...Don't Tell Me* on July 18, 2014. You can hear his interview at http://www.npr.org/2014/07/19/332570027/not-my-job-french-laundry-chef-thomas-keller-gets-quizzed-on-actual-laundry.

[17] Find information about the BJ Fogg's method of behavior change at www.foggmethod.com.

[18] Nichole Kelley, "Autodesk Scores a Home Run with Gamification," Social Media Explorer, November 8, 2012, http://www.socialmediaexplorer.com/social-media-

measurement/autodesk-scores-a-home-run-with-gamification.

[19] Scott, *The New Rules of Sales and Service*, page 14.

[20] Daniel H. Pink, *To Sell Is Human: The Surprising Truth About Moving Others*, Riverhead Books (2012), p. 226.

[21] Dan Ariely, "What's the Value of a Big Bonus?" *New York Times*, November 19, 2008.

[22] Simon Mainwaring, *We First: How Brands and Consumers Use Social Media to Build a Better World*, St. Martin's Press (2011).

[23] Justin Kirkham, "Blizzard Targets Busy Gamers, Students in World of Warcraft Expansion," The Arbiter Online, August 25, 2014, http://arbiteronline.com/2014/08/25/blizzard-targets-busy-gamers-students-in-world-of-warcraft-expansion.

[24] Cone Communications, *2013 Cone Communications Social Impact Study*, available at http://www.conecomm.com/2013-social-impact.

[25] Carmine Gallo, "Your Story Is Your Strategy, Says VC Who Backed Facebook and Twitter," Forbes.com, April 29, 2014.

[26] Unilever Sustainable Living Plan Summary, Unilever website, http://www.unilever.com/images/slp_Unilever-Sustainable-Living-Plan-2013_tcm13-388693.pdf.

[27] Ann Handley, *Everybody Writes: Your Go-To Guide to Creating Ridiculously Good Content*, Wiley (2014).

[28] Bernadette Jiwa, *Difference: The One-Page Method for Reimagining Your Business and Reinventing Your Marketing*, The Story of Telling Press (2014).

[29] Ty Montague, *True Story: How to Combine Story and Action to Transform Your Business*, Harvard Business Review Press (2013).

[30] Andrew S. Winston, *The Big Pivot: Radically Practical Strategies for a Hotter, Scarcer, and More Open World*, Harvard Business Review Press (2014).

[31] "IT Buyers to Vendors: 'It's Complicated' " ServiceSource press release, November 15, 2013.

[32] Net Promoter, Net Promoter Score, and NPS are trademarks of Satmetrix Systems, Inc., Bain & Company, Inc., and Fred Reichheld.

[33] The CMO Survey is sponsored by Duke Fuqua School of Business, American Marketing Association, and McKinsey, Inc. Find the latest results at cmosurvey.org.

[34] Joe Pulizzi, *Epic Content Marketing: How to Tell a Different Story, Break through the Clutter, and Win More Customers by Marketing Less*, McGraw-Hill Education (2014), page 3.

[35] MarketingProfs and Content Marketing Institute, "2015 B2B Content Marketing Trends – North America," http://www.marketingprofs.com/charts/2014/26154/2015-b2b-content-marketing-benchmarks-budgets-and-trends.

[36] Joe Pulizzi, *Epic Content Marketing*, page 290.

[37] Nadia Cameron, "Interview: Marketo CEO Phil Fernandez on customer expectations and competition," CMO.Com, August 22, 2014.

[38] Jonah Sachs, *Winning the Story Wars: Why Those Who Tell (and Live) the Best Stories Will Rule the Future*, Harvard Business Review Press (2012), page 86.

[39] Kathy Klotz Guest, "Lighten Up Your Marketing," *Keeping it Human* blog, August 27, 2014, http://keepingithuman.com/lighten-up-your-marketing.

[40] Cone Communications, *2013 Cone Communications Social Impact Study*, available at http://www.conecomm.com/2013-social-impact.

About the Author

Anne Janzer is an author, speaker, and marketing consultant with more than 20 years of experience working with high tech businesses. She has worked with over a hundred technology businesses, from industry giants like VMware to innovative start-ups like Box, to articulate positioning and messaging in crowded markets.

As a collaborative ghost writer for corporate executives, her work has appeared in dozens of industry publications and blogs, including Wired.com and the Sand Hill blog. She speaks about subscription marketing at industry events.

Anne is a graduate of Stanford University and lives in the Bay Area. She's working on her next book now.

Follow her on Twitter at @AnneJanzer, or on her blog at AnneJanzer.com. And if you liked this book, leave a review on Amazon.

To explore the topic of subscription marketing beyond the book, visit the Resources page on the book website: www.SubscriptionMarketingBook.com/resources. Enter your email to join the subscription marketing group and download related resources.

Made in the USA
San Bernardino, CA
17 November 2015